Social InSecurity

Social InSecurity

How to Survive the Coming Prosperity and Retire at Twice Your Final Salary

George M. Perry

Writer's Showcase presented by *Writer's Digest*

San Jose New York Lincoln Shanghai

Social InSecurity
How to Survive the Coming Prosperity and
Retire at Twice Your Final Salary

Published by Writer's Showcase presented by *Writer's Digest*
an imprint of iUniverse.com, Inc.

For information address:
iUniverse.com, Inc.
620 North 48th Street
Suite 201
Lincoln, NE 68504-3467
www.iuniverse.com

ISBN: 0-595-00293-5

Printed in the United States of America

To Anita—my wife, my muse, the "wind beneath my wings"

Epigraph

Today a hope of many years' standing is fulfilled...We can never insure one hundred percent of the population against one hundred percent of the hazards and vicissitudes of life, but we have tried to frame a law which will give some measure of protection to the average citizen and to his family againt the loss of a job and against poverty—ridden old age.

Franklin Delano Roosevelt,
upon signing the Social Security Act 8/14/1935

Although only 19 years old, the Chilean social pension program, despite its flaws, is earning a consistent 13% in each of its three conservatively managed portfolios. José Lunchbucket, who earns $10,000 a year, and will never save a peso on his own, can look forward to retiring on a pension worth up to **25 times** his annual wage. His American counterpart, earning near twice as much, but contributing an equivalent amount to Social Security, is guaranteed a pension worth almost **half** his modest pay. Yet we seem so content. It's enough to break your heart. Doesn't anyone care?

George M. Perry, *Social InSecurity* 2/2/2000

Table of Contents

Preface

The American people have a problem. A big problem. Their retirement. Older people worry about Social Security benefits being cut. Young people fear that Social Security will be 'gone' when they are old. Neither will happen. The real problem is that Social Security will not deliver the benefits it could and should to achieve the 21st Century goal of retiring at twice your final salary.

Social InSecurity describes in simple terms (with shortcut math), why the problem exists and what we must do to overcome it. It describes how Social Security must be modernized, and what you can do to help. And what you can do if Washington never catches on.

The American people have another major problem. It's called Medicare and costs are inexorably rising. There's even talk of rationing health care, of depriving very old people of life improving treatment on the grounds we can't afford it, and they're not going to last very long anyway. That's not civilized. Nor necessary. *Social InSecurity* tells you how this too, can change.

We have chosen electronic publication in order to present the most timely information possible and still have the book available before the presidential primaries are over. Normal schedules would have produced the book after the election, when the issues may well be moot. The politicians are treading gingerly around the Social Security mess. New Yorkers, 'the Donald' (Trump) and 'the Steve' (Forbes), are bold enough to criticize and to note the benefits of privatization. The Donald early-on recognized that SS is a Ponzi scheme (could we call this 'the Don's early right?') but then gets bogged down in palaver about the trust fund being fictitious. Just because the Trust trusts the government to honor its non-interest bearing IOU's doesn't make it non-existent. Trump shows considerable perspicacity in branding Clinton's idea of having the Government play the market as fallacious (there's a lot of that going around). Does he want them to dump the cash in a huge pile in the middle of the SSA's conference room (like the early days at Foxwoods— now there's a metaphor to make the Donald shudder)?

Everyone seems hung up on the 'guaranteed' SS pension. Since the average check is for less than $1000 a month, they are guaranteeing something for the millions that have no other pensions or savings. They are guaranteeing poverty. In a presidential campaign that is rapidly becoming a 'beauty contest' for wealthy men, these are real issues that should be heard. You can make it happen.

Acknowledgements

- Having escaped computers some 20 years ago, it is indeed ironic that I find myself involved in electronic publishing. Thank goodness the people at iUniverse were so patient and helpful. I am most indebted to my wife, Anita, who in addition to serving as confidant, editor, critic, proofreader, transcriber, and best friend, did yeoman service as Internet interface, 'pre-Pentium' laptop repair person, *WORD* and Internet maven. Thanks also to Jim Salvato for the fine Frontispiece illustration.

- I also appreciate the critical review and analysis performed by Lew Walter, CPA (and one of my favorite bridge partners); Delos Smith, economist for the Conference Board and CNBC (and other media) economics commentator; and Bill Mork, J.D., CPA, my accountant and tax lawyer.

Introduction

I first became interested in the Social Security 'problem' about 10 years ago. We had finally gotten our personal pension engine humming on all cylinders and we could look forward to retiring in 3 or 4 years.

At that time I was running a 'skunkworks' for my employer. We experimented with many product and marketing ideas. Our skunkworks group had sponsored several successful start-up operations for the company. Today these start-ups—in auto insurance, banking, and income tax preparation are thriving. Less successful were efforts to find new products and marketing methods for our traditional businesses, although our research into delivery systems led to a sweeping 're-engineering' of our sales force in 1994.

The pension arena is, of course, of critical importance to a financial services company. Retirement products became a special interest of mine. The concept of a privatized social security was just beginning to be bandied about in the early 90's and it caught my attention. Being of short attention span and caught up in a pre-retirement move to NYC, I didn't regain my focus until well after my retirement began.

I have tinkered with the probabilities of long term investment returns over the years (I'm one to tinker forever with chance) and thought that the 'time value of money' could save Social Security much as it saved my personal retirement plan. When I first wrote about 'Bill & Warren' they were worth only $50 billion. My focus became more intense this past summer and the book, after the initial two stage setting chapters, evolved as my thinking matured. You can follow the ideas as they develop.

You will note that I try to avoid ponderous, mind-numbing statistics and rely on the reader's common sense to lead him/her to a rational conclusion. I recently came upon new studies that maintain the median family income to be $40,000, which I dutifully plugged into my treatise, noting that the situation is worse than one would surmise. That same study maintained that 50% of America's families have less than $1000 in personal savings of all kinds. It excluded only net home equity and contributions to an employer's defined contribution pension plan. This is truly scary and suggests that the situation is far worse than I imagined. Yet I'm sure some Social Security apologists will claim I exaggerate.

The only 'optimistic' investment number used in this book is to project that 'good' equity mutual funds will return as much as the S&P 500 has over the past 20 years; about 15% with 3% inflation. There is, furthermore, no specific investment advice offered herein except to buy good equity mutual funds for your long-term retirement portfolio. This is hardly revolutionary.

Your author is not a registered investment advisor and, under SEC regulations, is not qualified to give specific investment advice. Your author is also not a licensed physician and is clearly not qualified to give medical advice. The investment and health care opinions presented herein are strictly those of the author. Any anticipated investment or health maintenance action should be thoroughly reviewed by your trusted investment advisor or your physician before proceeding.

Election year 2000 promises a lively campaign for the Presidency and much of Congress. Seldom in my memory have we had issues of real concern to everyone, especially the silent majority. All of us should have an abiding interest in our eventual retirement, the retirement of our children and grandchildren, and medical care for their golden years. If this book really gets you to think hard about Social Security, to take a stand and, hopefully, speak out, it will have achieved its purpose.

I. Setting the Stage

Time Value of Money

It is our intent to reach an agreement with you on what the world will look like, in general terms, 50 years hence, and help you optimize your personal and financial situation in light of expected events. You may have no plans to be around in 2050, in which case much of the benefit will accrue to your heirs. On the other hand, we may convince you that your longevity expectations are much too modest, even if you're now 60 years old. You might well see 110, and not necessarily from the vegetable bin.

This is not a super scientific or even pseudo scientific treatise, but merely the melding of probabilities, common sense and some basic mathematical givens. We'll not belabor you with mind numbing statistics but neither shall we manipulate the facts, in 'Limbough' fashion just to make our point. You must have, however, a thorough understanding of a few principles and if you are not comfortable with them you will be classified as hopelessly risk averse.

The key mathematical element is the 'time value of money.' This simply refers to the extraordinary effect of compound interest over time. An attractive interest rate and a healthy amount of time can do wonders to a given pot of money. The critical factor is the interest rate. The best way to understand the relative value of interest rates is to compute how long it will take your money to double at each interest rate. Simply divide 72 by the interest rate to find how long it will take for your money to double. Table 1, below, is well worth memorizing or at least understanding.

Table 1. The rule of 72

Interest Rate	# of years to double
2%	36
3%	24
4%	18
6%	12
8%	9
9%	8
12%	6
18%	4
24%	3
36%	2

Don't ask me why the rule of 72 works, it just does. You'll notice that in most of our examples we'll use one of these rates. It makes it so much easier to do the math in your head, or on your fingers. Here's a short-cut, double a dollar ten times and it becomes a thousand (a thousand doubled 10 times become a million). Thus 9 times is half a million, 8 times, a quarter million, and 7 times, is 125,000. Your fingers become 2,4,8,16,&32. A sixth finger would give you 64, or you can remember that 6 doubles equals (almost) 66.

The other side of the coin is the length of time it will take for inflation to cut your pot of gold in half (in purchasing power). Three percent inflation cuts your stash in half every 24 years; 2% inflation stretches it to 36 years. That old rule of 72 strikes again, only in reverse. To accurately portray the future, it's very important to express returns net of inflation, or in 'constant dollars.'

A simple illustration: You are 30 years old and received a windfall $10,000 from your Aunt Tillie's estate. Since you're worried about Social Security (but for all the wrong reasons), you wish to invest 'safely' for your retirement. You've heard that some mutual funds consistently return 12% or better but you decide it's OK to have half as much money at age 66 and sleep well for 36 years. So you buy 6% government bonds.

You're wrong on several levels and if you knew the facts, wouldn't sleep well either. In good safe government bonds your $10,000 will become $80,000 in 36 years (doubling in the 12th, 24th and 36th years) good for a couple years of modestly active retirement. But wait a minute. If inflation is only 3% (about right for the last decade) your $80,000 is worth less than half that amount, about $25,000 in today's money. Maybe one decent year of retirement. Interest rate minus the inflation rate is called the 'real rate of return.' Real rates of return should, of course, be used in calculating the real value of money at some future date.

Back to our example. Actually its worse that it appears. At 12% the alternative mutual fund investment of Aunt Tillie's $10,000 grows (doubling 6 times) into $320,000 by your 66th birthday. Wow! Twice the interest rate produces four times as much money. But what about inflation? Much to your dismay you find that the S & P 500 index funds have historically (over the last 25 years or so) produced returns that reach 15% or more and discounting 3% for inflation they produced a 12% or better real return. A top rated fund would produce near 18% net, if history repeats, but this number ($2,500,000) is surreal and beyond everyone's comprehension.

If all this is true, you could take your mutual fund kitty at age 66, and buy a life time annuity that will give you more money every year as long as you live, than the bond investment produces in a single lump sum.

The fund investment is not twice as productive as the bond investment as you initially surmised but is at least 10 times and might prove to be 20-30 times as productive! The 'time value of money' is a powerful ally. Yet you are willing to give this up in return for 36 years of delusional bed rest. Which leads us to our second major factor: risk.

Risk & Exposure

Most people, like you and me, are very risk averse when it comes to managing their money, and often less concerned when risking their lives. A rather extreme example is the Merrill Lynch commercial showing the daredevil hang gliding over the Grand Canyon. Now if he's in the top ten of the nation's hang gliders this year, it is because, as the saying goes, all of last year's top 10 have been killed. Yet he's so conservative in handing his money that only Merrill Lynch is up to the task. If they are advising him properly, every nickel should be in low cost term life insurance. Someone should get a bonanza out of his lunacy.

Although everyone is well aware of risk, rational understanding is rare. Risk is seldom quantified except that we're told that the higher the interest rate, the higher the risk premium. This is quite true in comparing the risk in an insured mortgage vs. the risk in loan sharking. But it has little to do with the risk in equities in general, and long term mutual funds in particular.

The risk factor in equities over the long haul is negligible. It can be stated simply in terms of probabilities. What is the probability that equities, over the long haul, will return less than 'safe' fixed investments? The probability that stocks will return less than 3-4% in real terms over the next few decades must be close to zero, especially if you accept the premise that the world will be at least a little better off 50 years hence. Rather than try to quantify risk precisely we will deal instead with probabilities. The probability of savings bonds outperforming stocks is extremely low. The probability of a 30's style depression is equally minuscule. The probability of a third world war is even more insignificant.

The other side of risk is exposure. The probability of something bad happening might be very low, but if you are frequently exposed to conditions conducive to the dire event, your risk can become quite high. To illustrate: the odds against being hit by lightning and being in a major auto accident are both, let us say, about 1 in 10,000. You are, however, exposed to auto accident risk every time you get into a car. Thus, in 10,000 days of getting into a car (about 30 years), you are odds on to get in a major accident. That's why you always buckle up. Your odds today are only 1 in 10,000 but you know that sooner or later your number should come up. Conversely, your real odds of getting hit by lightning are much less since you have relatively little exposure to lightning. Perhaps 100 days in a lifetime you're in serious harms way. A little common sense like staying off the golf course and you're relatively safe. If you agonize over the minuscule probability of a real crash and keep a portion of your long-term capital in fixed instruments, it is the risk equivalent of walking around with a lightening rod attached to your rump.

Critical Mass

Another concept we will explore is 'critical mass.' Critical mass is a somewhat amorphous term that defines when a phenomenon reaches real significance. I first worked with computers in 1954. Our giant (literally) computer, costing millions, had less internal storage than my current $50 Casio computer watch. But computers didn't achieve critical mass until well into the 80's, at which time their impact on all aspects of our lives exploded. At that time, economists lost what little ability they had to measure the computer's contribution to productivity [Their attempts to measure MIPS—millions of instructions per second—was patently absurd. MIPS never had any real relationship to actual accomplishment.] In the 90's, of course, computer utilization continued to grow exponentially with the ubiquitous PC's. Having achieved critical mass the computer impact—not only the obvious PC's, but zillions of tiny preprogrammed chips that seemingly infect every device made by man—will grow in ways that we are incapable of comprehending.

In 1975 I, like Al Gore, worked with Arpanet, a packet switching network that evolved into the Internet. Yet twenty years later when I again had Internet exposure, it had still not reached critical mass. We were working on an America On Line application, lamenting that it was too bad we couldn't get Prodigy, the leader, to work with us. In those days, the Internet was primarily chat rooms, porn, and dull newspaper substitutes. As my wife Anita would say, the habitat of "infomaniacs." It had not reached critical mass. But it did so a few years later as the useful applications exploded. We can only guess at what the ultimate potential may be. We don't need to know. But it will be huge.

There are a number of phenomena that are worthy of a critical mass analysis. Since we know that growth is explosive once critical mass is reached, it is important to try to assess whether it has been achieved or is yet to happen. We'll explore the critical mass of the following key aspects of our analysis of the next half-century.

Longevity—life expectancy back in the year '0000' was about 25-30 years. 1900 years later it was about 50. Not much progress there. But in the ensuing 100 years it increased 50%. Has the explosion started? What are the consequences if it has?

Health Care—Much of the improvement in longevity is due to advances in health care. Much of our political rhetoric is directed at health care cost. Have we reached the pinnacle?

Commerce and Economic System Management—Has globalization peaked? Will eCommerce be really significant? Is there a reason why recessions have become less severe and less frequent? Have we reached the point where we can truly control the economy?

Militarism—Don't look now but we've achieved world domination to a degree that would make the most megalomaniacal dictator proud. Has the technology of warfare reached, or passed, its peak?

Crime Prevention—Does DNA foretell a new era in criminal prosecution? Does technology suggest a new paradigm?

'S' Curves

The life cycle of a business, or industry, is sometimes described as an 'S' curve. The McKinsey consulting firm popularized the 'S' curve phenomena. If there are any of them around your shop you might ask them to explain 'S' curves. You might even distract them enough that they forego an opportunity to examine your cubical too closely.

Baring that, I could attempt an explanation. When a company starts out, its growth chart typically shows a slow and steady upward movement.Then, if it catches on, it achieves critical mass, and the trend line shoots upward. Inevitably, it will mature and the growth line flattens out. Eventually, as the theory goes, it will turn downward, and, if the company doesn't reinvent itself and jump off the downward slope (presumably with McKinsey's help) it will atrophy and die.

A classic example of 'S' curves is the sailing ship industry. Sailing ships blossomed in the 17th century and achieved critical mass in the early 19th century when Britain ruled the waves. They boomed as the primary vehicle of commerce until the steamship made its appearance. The sailing ships were doomed. During the last 10 years of their existence they made more technological strides than in all the previous centuries of sailing ship evolution. But it was hopeless. The best sailing ship was not as effective as the worst steamship. By the beginning of the 20th century, sailing ships were no longer used for commerce.

Conversely, an excellent example of an industry jumping off the 'S' curve and reinventing itself is the vacation cruise business. The great transatlantic ocean liners, Queens Mary and Elizabeth, the United States, the France and others reached their zenith before WWII, served nobly during the conflagration, and returned to glory afterward.

It was but fifteen years before the jets drove the liners into bankruptcy. Yet out of the rubble rose the cruise ships. Cunard, the only transatlantic company that truly survived, made its QEII dual purpose: summer trips across the Atlantic, winters in the Caribbean. The France became the Norway, the Rotterdam hung on, but by and large the liners faded away, to be replaced by Carnival fun ships. I had it all brought home to me, sailing on the Vistafjord one foggy day as we dawdled through the Dardanelles on our way to Yalta when out of the mist loomed a huge gray apparition being towed by two menacing tugboats.

It was the 'United States,' the fastest liner ever built. Her massive engines strangely silent, she slid mournfully by, headed for an anonymous Turkish port. Workers there, uninformed (or unconcerned) about asbestos, were waiting to strip the vile substance from her innards. The latest buyer had invested a purported $150,000 in her purchase and was planning to spend $40 million more to rebuild all but the hull and the awesome engines. That was 1993 and the 'United States' hasn't been heard from since. The cruise liner business has already surpassed the mordant passenger liner business and will not reach critical mass until all baby boomers reach the 'age of cruising.'

Currently there are several industries sliding down the slippery slope of their 'S' curve toward oblivion. It's not so much that the industries will disappear, like the proverbial buggy whip manufacturers, but that they will cease to grow, will atrophy and many well-known companies will disappear through merger. Does Internet trading suggest that the traditional stock brokerage firm is on that slippery downward 'S' curve slope? They seem to be repositioning themselves as financial planners. Can the leopard change his spots?

The once proud life insurance industry is clearly one whose time has passed. When the public began to understand "buy term and invest the difference," the insurance industry could have reinvented itself as the investment advisor to America. Trouble is, most insurance companies clung to their traditions and even when they embraced financial planning the plan invariably said, "you need more insurance"—ending their credibility. For decades the life insurance industry owned health care, through insured medical plans. When HMO's and 'managed care' arrived, where were they? Stubbornly defending their traditional turf.

Titans like The Metropolitan and The Prudential struggled to regain their footing. They plunged into auto insurance with dubious results, the Pru tried stock brokerage acquisition with painful results, and both eventually lost out in the health care arena. Class action law suits claiming misrepresentation of life policies as retirement vehicles cost them millions and did little for their 'solid as the rock' reputations. Many mutual life companies found themselves locked out of capital access by their very structure and decided to become stock companies. It didn't make much difference.

Aetna Life and The Travelers were the twin towers of the multi-line insurance companies. The pillars of Hartford deteriorated almost in lock step with the decline and fall of the city itself, though it's difficult to see how the two were connected. The Travelers, drifting for years, was finally undone by the commercial real estate debacle of the 80's. Desperate for the big returns that declining interest rates no longer offered, they bought Texas towers that nobody wanted to occupy. Sandy Weill caught the Travelers as it was running into the ground. He sold off the once vaunted Group Insurance operation, bought the Aetna's declining Property and Casualty business, merged it with similar Travelers operations and spun them off into a separate subsidiary.

All that was left was a modest life insurance business, a good name and a few dozen red umbrellas. Sandy then merged in his collection of cats and dogs (Commercial credit, Associated Madison Insurance, Shearson and Smith Barney brokers, and the Al Williams horde of term insurance hustlers). The resulting combination took the Travelers good name, much to the consternation of old time Travelers agents, who suffered great discomfort when regulators cited Williams agents for their high sleaze factors and called them Traveler's agents. So much for good name. The resulting hybrid made lots of money, however, which allowed Sandy to pull off the Grand Coup: the merger with Citicorp. Although the Citicorp name was chosen for the new entity, Sandy was clearly the 'mergor,' John Reid, the 'mergee.'

The Aetna, meanwhile, tried to reinvent itself as the nations premier health care company. They sold off most everything except managed care and used the money to buy one of the slick new HMO outfits. It's very difficult to be premier in an industry that everyone hates. It's also difficult to make money consistently when the government spends a great deal of its limited energy trying to force you to make less money. Has the Aetna reinvented itself or gone from frying pan to fire?

The banking industry seems determined to follow a path of self-destruction. It all started with the ubiquitous ATM's that reached critical mass a few years ago. The ATM's were their salvation. The rising teller costs and the 'bricks and mortar' to support them were eating the banks alive. But within the savior were the seeds of destruction. With ATM's on every corner who needs to go to the bank? How then do they attract customers to their new investment and loan products? As a final insult, the public is demanding that banks not be allowed an ATM fee for dispensing money to non-customers. This is totally unfair—why should banks give free service to the enemy's customers?

If that weren't enough traditional banking businesses are headed south. Changes in the mortgage business killed the Savings and Loan Industry (how's that for an 'S' curve saga?) And will eventually do in the commercial banks. In the future, consumers will join with other consumers of like characteristics to form giant pools of money that will be shopped globally, abetted by the Internet, for the lowest interest rate. We'll talk more about pooling under eCommerce. In essence, banks that develop a fee business (mortgage servicing, payroll servicing and the like) will survive. Banks that stick to their knitting (loans and deposits) will be merged and re-merged in waves of consolidation.

On a smaller scale, the camera film business seems doomed. The digital camera will ultimately devour Kodak's film business. Picture this: In a few years you'll be carrying around with you a tiny $100 digital camera, with zoom lens and very high resolution (2 million pixels or more).You'll take pictures whenever the mood strikes; after all they cost nothing. When the magazine is full (50) you'll dump it into your PC and review the results. Some you'll immediately 'throw away' by wiping them out in memory. Others you might store in your archives for future reference. Still others you might E-mail to some of your friends and relatives. Still no cost. You might really like a couple and print them out (cost 25 cents each). Or you might assemble a bunch into a full-page collage and print it out (cost 50 cents).

How can Kodak (or Fuji, or Polaroid) compete? Can't. Kodak has effectively acknowledged this by offering photo CD's along with pictures when your film is developed. They promote the idea of loading the photo CD onto your PC and E-mailing copies of pictures to friends and relatives. Think about it: you buy film ($5), have it developed ($10), request a photo disk ($X), wait a week or two and you have what a digital camera gives you free and instantly. As long as digital cameras are $300, the Kodak photo CD will attract some business. But aren't they more likely to get people interested in digital photography and drive them to digital when the price point ($100?) precipitates critical mass? Sure Kodak will get its share of camera sales, but they've already lost much of that market to Japan. How rich can you get making $100 cameras? Their past attempts to broaden their base (chemicals, etc.) have not been happy marriages. The downward slope of their 'S' curve seems relentless and unforgiving. Their film business will not totally die. But growth will end and then gradual erosion will set in. Unless they can jump off their curve, reinvent themselves as something else, they will become a much more modest company than they are today.

A popular investing technique involves purchasing stock in the 5 Dow Jones Industrial Average stocks with the lowest P/E and the highest dividend pay out. It's called 'dogs of the Dow' and works pretty well. The theory is that they can't get much worse and at least one of the five should rebound from its slump, giving a reasonable return for the group. In our thinking, too many of the Dow 30 are dogs, although four were dumped in '97 and four more in late '99. These dogs are all examples of companies that are on the downside of their 'S' curves. Take a look at the entire 30 Dow stocks. How many do you think have put their best days behind them and are slowly sliding toward oblivion? If you are an investor in individual stocks, (not that we advocate doing such), you should avoid the suspect stocks, regardless of their dividends, in your long-term portfolio.

Peter Lynch tells us that if we really like a product, buy the stock. A friend of ours loves Boston Market (neé Boston Chicken), the only fast food chain in *Zagat*. He bought a lot of stock. They serve good quality food at low prices. Big problem—making money. They went bankrupt; are now owned by McDonalds. Their stock is worthless. Our friend is worth less. Better you should buy good mutual funds, put them under to mattress, and rest well.

II. The Future

From Zero to 2000 in a few Pages

Our first economic law is that each century is better than the previous. Not too profound, seems almost intuitive. But let's examine this premise a little closer. The first 15 or so centuries in calendar time produced little of value. Each dreary century during the dark ages was just as dreary as the previous hundred years. Man was getting smarter and more civilized, but he had little to show for it. Measurable progress didn't really begin until the advent of industrialization. It is not hard to accept that each century since then has been better than its predecessor. But perhaps a little more precision in our measurement is called for.

Let's look at recent half centuries. The second half of the 19th century was significantly better than 1800-1849. In spite of a horrific civil war (which rid us of a major impediment—slavery—to our claim to be a civilized nation) the move westward and rampant industrialization brought us into the community of first world countries.

At the beginning of the 20th century, the 'average' American family had no car, no indoor toilet, no radio, no household appliances (—washing machine, dryer, toaster, refrigerator, vacuum cleaner), and many had no electricity, phone, nor even running water. Then came a horrible 50 years. First a devastating world war, worse than the sum of all proceeding wars. The smoke had barely cleared from WWI when the world was struck by the mother of all flu seasons. The epidemic of 1918 killed twenty million people. Today we're aghast (and rightly so) when a plane crash kills 200. Can you visualize 100,000 planes crashing in one year? I can't.

The 20's were the golden days of this half-century filled with false prosperity and speculative excess. It all came crashing down in 1929 and we were cursed with the worst economic depression the modern world has ever seen—10 years of dreary misery. In 1939 we were rescued from universal poverty by "the war to end all wars"—WWII. It wasn't, but it was so horrific and all consuming that it made WWI seem a skirmish by comparison. At the end of the half-century, the world was still recovering from 100 million dead and the utter destruction of big chunks of the civilized world. The uncivilized world was relatively untouched.

Yet, in 1950 the average American family had radio, TV, electricity, indoor toilets, telephone, washer, drier, refrigerator, freezer, range, oven, maybe a dishwasher, and most likely a reliable car. The greatest gain in living standard of any half century since the beginning of the industrialized world occurred during fifty years of unbelievable turmoil and massive destruction. Incidentally, is the way you live in 2000 really all that different from 1950?

Purists might tell you that the really big gains were solidified during the fifties and were essentially a part of the first 50 years. To some extent this is true. History doesn't really fall into neat 50-year blocks. I personally feel that 1960-2000 does constitute the second half of the 20th Century. The fifties were really a continuation of the halcyon postwar years.

But, what matter. There's no question that the world is somewhat better off in 2000 than in 1950. No cold war, no 'real' wars of any kind. Vietnam, it turned out, was the "war that ended all wars." Why? Because it was on television. The whole world suddenly realized that war was not glamorous and generally a bad deal for all concerned.

Economically we find a muddy picture. Pundits tell us that starting in 1960 productivity plummeted to about 1% a year and stayed there until well into the 90's. The baby boomers are, we're told, the first generation that earns less, in real earning power, than their parents. The savings rate went to hell and never returned. The balance of payments never did balance. The dollar declined in value against major currencies. There were several significant recessions, although each seemed to have a shorter life and impact than the previous downturns.

If all this weren't bad enough for the beleaguered boomers, the real estate market turned on them, too. Much of their parents' net worth, it seems, came from appreciation in their homes. But after the last real estate crash, prevailing wisdom was that the honeymoon was over; never again could one get rich by just living in the right house. Although some see a new housing boom, it follows that if we continue to have low inflation, housing costs should not skyrocket.

But was it really as grim as it seems? Although no one was saving anything, the real value of all the equities in the stock market increased some 2000%. Yes, that's 20 to 1. Since no one was saving, who owned all that stock? Just rich people? Not likely, but maybe a bit disproportionately. But the old rich, children of the depression, know that stocks were bad. Maybe the young rich? Maybe lots of people, many of them worker bees owned stocks, with big chunks of money going into 401K's and IRA's as the revered but dreadful defined benefit pension plans begin to wane.

There seems little question that as the new millennium approaches (January 1, 2001) we are arguably approaching unprecedented prosperity. During the last half century, it appeared that productivity stalled and savings ceased. But, as we've noted elsewhere, it was the measuring that was faulty, not the reality.

The wealth of the nation has grown twenty-fold over the last half century. Wring out whatever inflation there was in equity (i.e. higher P/E ratios) and real estate values and it still was huge. Even though a disproportionate share went to the very wealthy, millions upon millions have shared in the largesse.

It is sad, indeed, that so many of the working poor (those who never enjoy 'disposable income') have not participated. The irony is that they could have so easily done so, had we enacted the Social Security reforms described herein back in 1960. You may say that's hindsight. Who could have known in 1960 that the Ponzi scheme old age assistance program designed for the 30's would eventually crash? It would seem that some actuary could have figured it out. But obviously no one did. Far more important is the fact that even though the needed reforms are patently obvious, the likelihood that they will be enacted is not overwhelming. The most likely 'reform' is to reduce benefits and dump more money into Social Security to stave off its bankruptcy a few more years. And in 2050 some nut will write a book lamenting why we didn't change the system back in 2000 so that all working people could have enjoyed a happy and healthy retirement.

Longevity and Health Care

Some people have lived to be 100 since the beginning of recorded history. But not many. It wasn't until the 20th Century that centurions became common. In the 21st century healthy people with good genes who reach 50, will have excellent odds for reaching 100. Health care has achieved critical mass during the last half century and cures are breaking out all over. If you watch the 11 PM news (10 central), you'll agree that hardly a day goes by without some breakthrough or medical miracle being breathlessly bantered about. Certainly some of the 'cures' prove less than miraculous and some of the procedures frivolous or cosmetic. Nonetheless, 200 or so breakthroughs a year is pretty awesome. Can you think of a better way to keep score?

Healthcare has gotten horribly expensive. And, it is getting even more so. Perhaps not the double-digit growth of the 80's, but costs do inexorably move upward. Back in the 70's, we blamed the doctors. They seemed to live just a little too well and besides, they wouldn't make house calls. In the 80's, the major employers became impatient with rising insurance costs and encouraged the formation of HMO's.

For a while, the HMO's made money and got a better spin by referring to themselves as 'managed care.' The doctor business went south. Older practitioners couldn't sell their practice; younger MD's took HMO jobs and 'punched a clock.' Then the roof fell in. Oxford, the high flier almost bellied, Aetna wasn't in great shape either. And yet, there was constant public (and congressional) yammer to hold down premiums. And, as usual, Medicare costs were going through the roof.

No one seems to want to admit that staying healthy simply is getting more expensive. All the miracle cures and procedures cost, big time, and aren't going to get much cheaper. Any time technology is involved; the costs will go down, yet utilization may increase to compensate. For example, many of us are accustomed to having our dentist routinely take full mouth x-rays before even poking around our mouth. Before too long, in a similar vein, your physician will order a MRI if you have a runny nose.

My doctor tells me that I'm going to get a new MRI type scan called Ultrafast-CT as soon as the local hospital has the machine installed. It can, in 10 minutes, provide a more complete analysis of the heart and all its arteries than the dreaded angiogram produced in what seemed hours.

There is one aspect of health care that technology has, but society has not, advanced far enough to deal with properly. Every year thousands of people die after waiting in vain for an appropriate body organ—heart, liver, kidney, lungs—to become available from a willing donor. Every year millions of appropriate organs are buried with their less willing owners. Will pig's organs someday fill the gap? Perhaps, but it doesn't seem likely. Could PR campaigns induce enough citizens to magnanimously sign donor cards? Probably not—there is no real incentive, no reason strong enough to compel people to look beyond the negative significance of the event (their own demise) and the 'ickiness' of the procedure to make this generous offer.

A more sophisticated society might respond to the need for incentive in a manner consistent with the tenets of a capitalistic world: money. It could work something like this. A person could for a pittance buy an insurance policy that paid his heirs a princely sum, let's say $50,000 if, upon his death, his organs, his corneas, ample amounts of skin, indeed, everything but the squeal, were successfully harvested. For many a needy family, it would be an effective alternative to life insurance.

The cost of transplant surgery is high. But that is not the issue. It is not that a $50,000 operation would now cost $75,000. The unavailability of organs at any cost is the real issue. Didn't eBAY almost auction off a kidney for several million dollars? Someone must develop a health insurance system capable of coping with the demands of 'endless life' (see Catastrophic Health Care—Chapter VIII).

Would 'organ insurance' somehow be immoral, be contrary to public policy? Might some heirs do in their benefactor in order to collect the 'organ jackpot'? No more so than ordinary life insurance, wherein occasionally heirs do, do in benefactors to collect the death benefit. Since the organ benefit is relatively modest compared to the levels of life insurance that tend to precipitate mayhem, one might conclude that donor insurance, that provides for young families upon the premature death of the breadwinner and, in addition, saves the lives of one or more other people (heart, kidney, liver) and improves the quality of life for even more (cornea, skin grafts) is far more consistent with enlightened public policy than ordinary life insurance.

Modern medicine has reached a pinnacle, even though there is still much to be done to find cures for many of our most dread diseases. But, the emphasis will change in the 21st century. The baby boomers are rapidly becoming seniors and the seniors before them have had a disproportionate effect on our public policy. The combination will clearly dominate and their agenda will be simple: aging, its cure and its prevention.

Conventional wisdom tells us to enjoy our fourscore and ten, if we're really lucky, and then check out. Don't make waves; don't try to live longer than you're supposed to. It is almost immoral to want to live indefinitely. Imagine the consternation at the Social Security Administration if this sort of thing caught on. Out the window go the actuarial tables and its bankruptcy city for the SSA.

It's going to happen. Genetic breakthroughs are just around the corner. Even more significant is the fact that people can manage their life expectancy in much the same way they manage their finances. You may yourself have a personal financial advisor; a financial planner, broker, CPA, perhaps an insurance agent with a broad perspective. Typically, you would pay the person an annual stipend to help your reach the proper decisions in managing your money against a predetermined set of goals. You may pay this person a lump sum, or with commission income, or an agreed upon combination or both. A key ingredient in your financial plan is an assumption of life expectancy.

In the future you may (some of us do it now) retain a physician as a health manager. This goes far beyond being conscientious about an annual physical exam. For starters, your physician should be a specialist in aging or planning to become so certified. There are less than 150 such specialists in the country today, and there may well be none in your area as it is a relatively new specialty. A physician whose philosophy is that aging is a disease, not something that is inevitable, will suffice. While aging is perhaps not curable at this point, it can be put in remission for many, many years.

The science of aging is still in its infancy; it may not reach critical mass until well into the new century. Although some aging therapies range between voodoo and the health food store, there are some well-grounded beliefs that consistently have a salutary effect in retarding 'fogginess' (as in 'old fogy'). You may have heard of a drug called Selegiline. It is not pasta, but a proven ally in the fight against Parkinson's disease. Long ago the patents expired, so there is little incentive to further research the compound. But Selegiline has shown remarkable 'side affects' that appear to retard aging. Pfizer's veterinary division has received FTC approval for a doggy version that revitalizes old dogs. So if you're an 'old dog' who wants a more lustrous fur and a pinker tongue, ask your medical advisor about Selegilene.

DHEA is a popular 'moss retardant' but you should use the very expensive prescription 'micronized' version rather than health food store varieties for best results. Currently, the most promising (and expensive) therapy is HGH (Human Growth Hormone) which is used primarily to help dwarfed children grow more normally, and by athletes who want to illegally build up their bodies. HGH is a natural hormone (and it can't easily be determined if an athlete is mainlining or is naturally youthful) produced by the pituitary to make you grow. After age 21 or so, the pituitary says "enough already," since your reproductive years will soon be in decline, as will your natural production of HGH, as will you. Mother Nature abhors the vacuous.

Although it may not be nice, you can fool Mother Nature by taking carefully monitored shots of HGH at upwards of $1000 per month. We never said living forever would be cheap, not at this point, anyway. If you feel someone should reimburse you for all your medical expenses, maybe living forever is not for you. I'm sure some of you may pay your financial advisor a couple thousand a year without a whimper or reimbursable dime, but you'll probably blanch at the thought of paying a medical advisor a similar sum. And don't expect your HMO (or even more so, Medicare) to show any sympathy.

Is HGH unequivocally proven effective and completely safe? Not yet, although all signs, thus far, appear positive. However, it can be misused and cause mischief. Although a promising immune system booster, HGH, showing no partiality, might help certain tumors grow. Thus, the complete diagnostics and 'engine' check-up before you start. But a conclusive double blind study? Not likely. Can you imagine 100 septuagenarians injecting HGH every day and another 100 codgers mainlining a placebo every day for 30 years and then comparing survival rates? You should live so long. If all this bothers you, maybe you shouldn't.

Do not be misled by the thought that longevity is the province of only the rich. We can all do a decent job of managing our finances ourselves with a little research, conscientious study and effort and do nearly as well as a professional manager. Similarly, a student of aging can learn enough and follow an exercise, diet and vitamin regimen that can accomplish a great deal. It won't be inexpensive (Fred Flintstone chewables are not adequate) but it can be well within the means of anyone who places high priority on a long, healthy life. HGH is a bit pricey, but in a few years it might well be down to $100 a month and not require injections. By then the hypothalamic hormone that stimulates pituitary GH production (GHRH), may be more widely available and less expensive. How do I know all this? From our son, Steve, who is arguably the leading 'civilian' expert on anti-aging. In the meantime, before the big breakthrough, you can do wonders with diet, exercise and age 'retardants' such as DHEA, Melatonin and Selegiline. After consulting your own physician, of course.

One of this book's goals is to convince you that you can and should retire at twice or more your salary at peak earning years. No more of this "half salary is enough" nonsense. A second major goal is that the healthy part of your retirement should last as long or longer than your total working life. To make this happen, you may need a healthy piece of that double salary to pay for your share of immortality. But hopefully we'll discover millenium solutions for millenium babies becoming Methuselahs. We've added a chapter (VIII) on a new health care paradigm for a new century.

War in the 21st Century

A cursory review of war in the 20th Century suggests that the world is getting smarter, albeit at a most moderate pace.

The first big one, WWI, was probably history's most futile war in terms of significant changes per million bodies. As far as I can tell, very little was accomplished. Surely it sowed the seeds of the monstrous Third Reich and signaled the start of the decline of France and Britain as world powers, but these are by-products. The war itself accomplished little. The United States emerged as a world leader and championed the idea that countries should be nice and treat each other civilly. Something we still do, much to the consternation of those citizens with a more insular mentality.

WWII, as we are incessantly told, was the most justified war ever. Certainly the Nazi menace had to be destroyed for it is hard to imagine it co-existing on a civilized planet. The Japanese were ambitious, paranoid, misguided, but not nearly as venal. After their militarism was extracted, both countries were gradually allowed to return to the community of nations. Both are military eunuchs, however, with little ability to ever flex any military muscle.

One real consequence of WWII was to forever emasculate the only two countries legitimately capable of competing with the United States for technological military leadership and eventual world domination. To compete in this arena, a nation must have a leading edge, engineering oriented educational system, a strong, incentive driven economy and a burning desire to compete. Japan and Germany had all these attributes, but losing WWII put them permanently on the sidelines.

The Cold War lasted over 40 years, until the pretender to world technological leadership collapsed. Russia had the brainpower, cultural orientation and at the top, at least, the burning desire. The Russians did produce some technological miracles, enough so to get us up off our complacent rumps, but also produced a lot of 'Woolworth' quality armaments.

It may well be that Reagan's fatuous Star Wars strategy was the last straw. The Russian economy apparently was always on the brink of collapse (shouldn't someone have noticed?) and trying to keep up with Star Wars did them in. All of this was not lost on the rest of the world, who are content to steal as many of our technology secrets as they can as a means of keeping up. I sometimes wonder if we don't relax security occasionally so that our potential adversaries don't get too paranoid about falling behind.

The 'warm' wars in the second half of the 20th Century were ugly affairs. The Korean War may have been necessary. One interesting observation (again, not lost on the world community) was that pre-Korean war, the South was the poor, agrarian part of Korea while the North was the more affluent and industrialized. After the war, the U.S. underwrote the South Korean recovery. The communists, concurrently, put the North Korean economy in the toilet. There is currently no country of any significance that thinks that communist dogma is a sound basis for economic policy.

North Korea may well be a real threat, in that they have ballistic missiles of some consequence. However, these are the same folks that built a colossal, showcase hotel in downtown Pyongyang to show the world that North Korea was not to be trifled with. A full hundred stories high, the colossus never opened. Seems that the northerners didn't fully comprehend the significance of the word 'plumb.' The building was so lopsided, the elevator shafts were so out of plumb that the elevators could go but a few floors before getting stuck. These are the people that are going to threaten us with missiles. Said missiles are courtesy of the Soviets, the original gang that couldn't shoot missiles straight (Scud).

The last major 20th Century war was the Vietnam debacle. You have only to crawl through the Cuchi Tunnels as we did (in 1992, thankfully, not 1972) to realize how frustrating and futile it is to line up with the wrong side, facing a determined, driven and implacable foe. Vietnam was clearly the ugliest war and, thanks to Ted Turner, everyone, around the globe, saw it unfold on the evening news. Vietnam totally de-glamorized war and made it very unpopular as a means of furthering jingoistic goals.

In the 70's and 80's it began to dawn on the nations of the world that the only war worth fighting was the economic war. Countries who had jettisoned shrill ideologies in favor of a pragmatic market driven economy were beginning to prosper. So what if they were a little impatient with democratic principles and civil rights. Prosperity first, then democracy, seemed a better approach than trying to ladle democracy onto a dreadful economy, à la India, which is improving, but at such a painfully slow rate.

One of the major accomplishments of the 20th Century was the achievement of self-sufficiency by all of the major nations of the world. Self sufficiency in terms of developing their agrarian economies (through technology) to the point that they could feed their own people. They could then turn their attention to developing an export capability, with the USA the target market.

China is developing a thriving market economy and we already have a serious balance of payments problem with them. Amazing what a few Christmas ornaments can do. Although China rattles a lot of swords, it is too rational to precipitate a military confrontation with the U.S. War, consequently, became the province of the lunatic fringe. Sadam Hussain built an army third only to China and the U.S., and marched into Kuwait. Kuwait has oil, which gave them the high moral ground.

When we demurred, Sadam promised us the "mother of all battles." As we assembled our 'desert storm' retaliatory ground forces, our technological superiority made it obvious that Sadam's venture would be thwarted. His vaunted high tech cannon lobbed shells from an incredible distance. Yet, our computers quietly computed the trajectory of

Sadam's shells, and dispatched missiles to follow the trajectory back to its source. Pretty soon, no more big guns. This story may well be allegorical but it underscores the inevitability of our technology grinding down any advisory. Was it one day or two after ground troops made contact with Sadam's elite that the Iraqis broke ranks and ran?

Except for one errant SCUD missile (otherwise a laughable weapon) our losses were minimal. Sadam's army was crushed with, sadly, a huge loss of life. It almost seemed that we could have prevailed without ground troops.

The world learned that one doesn't covet thy neighbor's oil wells. Yet to be learned was that it is not tolerable for first world countries to have civil wars, especially if they are conducted in an unseemly manner.

The brief war in Kosovo was most instructional for any observant country. Although there was great clamor for ground troops, the war ended without a single NATO battle casualty. Ground troops were irrelevant. We conducted a remote control war, with only a few pilots in harms way. Are we more than a generation away from when all offensive weapons will be 'unmanned'?

The world now knows that if we are severely irked we can sit back and systematically destroy the 'irker.' We can rain Cruise missiles (or more likely their progeny) on them, at a most leisurely pace, with no losses of our own, until the adversary is ruined. How likely is it that any significant opponent will risk seriously irking us? The chance of a major conflagration in the next 50 years approaches nil.

All this suggests a better quality of life for the nation in the next half century, and for many, a better quantity as well. War, the cause of the worst U.S. inflation of the 20th century will, consequently, not be a factor over the next 50 years, further reducing the likelihood of serious inflation (and the concomitant economic disruption) in the century ahead.

An even greater benefit is possible. Think about it: we can now conduct a significant military operation with no foot soldiers, no casualties. A 'Kosovo' type operation could quell any belligerence by the likes of

North Korea, Iran, Iraq or any other fringe operation that might challenge us. It is the ultimate war of attrition. We only need be patient.

In the 20th Century we debated women in the Army, gays in the Army. In the 21st Century we should debate people in the Army. That's right, who needs an army? A fast strike ground force is available (primarily as a deterrent) through the Marine Corps. We would still need a navy, to move our missiles and drones around the world, and an air force. One might think the Navy air force would be sufficient, but it's unlikely we can persuade one of our air forces to pack it in.

Reducing our military personnel from 3 million to 2 million people would save, I would guess $50 billion or more each year. It costs nearly $50,000 to keep someone in prison for a year. A soldier has all the benefits of a convict, in addition to drawing a salary. Come to think of it, in a high tech world why on earth would anyone wish to maintain a military force of even two million people?

The Army recently announced it would recruit high school dropouts because enlistments were down. Obviously this is the wrong answer. If all the Army jobs that can be filled by dropouts were left unfilled, what would be the loss? For that matter, if all Army recruiting were to cease, what would be the loss? It would seem, in recent warfare, foot soldiers have become an anachronism. Cannon fodder is passé. The Clinton administration has all but admitted that, unless national security is threatened, the American people will not tolerate any interventions that involve ground forces and casualties. Is it possible that the Pentagon, in its rush to replenish the ranks of its giant army, has an agenda we're unaware of?

It's clear that our military of the future should be primarily a cadre of high-tech mechanics and operators. The Marine Corps would provide the shock troops and our NATO allies, or better yet, third world UN members would provide the peacekeeping forces. It could be their primary source of export hard currency. It is in our best interests, even in the narrowest sense, to support the UN as the world's policemen.

We are not suggesting that the 21st century will be Shangri-La for everyone, with eternal peace and prosperity. Far from it. There will be many civil wars, internecine warfare and probably some massive genocide, although one would hope that Rwanda was the last such horror. It will probably be the 22nd century before we can say we have truly banished war.

The end of major wars as we know them means a more stable economy, removal of a significant 'trade barrier,' lower likelihood of inflationary pressures and the opportunity to save enough in military budgets to pay for a big piece of a relevant privatized Social Security.

Crime in the 21st Century

Violent crime is down, across the continent. Down to levels we haven't seen since the '60's. And it seems to be steadily receding. Why?

Conventional wisdom has it that prosperity lowers crime. That makes sense; good times mean lower unemployment, thus less despair, less hunger. Prosperity certainly takes some credit. Fewer teenagers (perhaps courtesy of the abortion boom of the 70's) is also noted as a primary reason for lower crime. Since teenagers are disproportionately represented among the miscreant, the current demographic probably has an impact. But I would like to cite two other factors that I feel have a significant impact on crime statistics.

• Draconian Drug Laws

It's difficult to have much crime when 'everybody' who's so inclined is already in jail. Our Draconian drug laws throw anyone in jail that dares 'crack' a smile. Many don't deserve the harsh sentences for some rather modest drug crimes. But the 600,000 or so incarcerated for drug offenses probably represent a demographic with a rather high proclivity toward crime—certainly a substantially higher propensity than a randomly selected group of 600,000 citizens. Many potential career criminals are being locked up for long stretches for abusing drug laws and don't get a chance to do much damage.

• Technology

I feel there is one factor that is reducing crime and will continue to do so, at an increasing rate. The greatest impact on crime in the 21st Century is just beginning to show significant impact and may well reach critical mass in the next decade or two. That factor is, as you might have guessed, technology.

DNA evidence is just beginning to achieve real significance. The DNA of all convicted felons will soon be readily accessible by law enforcement. And we all know that most violent crime (other than domestic disputes) is perpetrated by repeat felons. In a few years we will, moreover, get over the privacy nonsense that makes presumed law abiding citizens rail against providing government with their DNA samples. The ACLU and we got over finger printing as an innate evil; in time, this too shall pass.

Not overly bright people commit most violent crime. But the word will get around—"the weed of crime bears bitter fruit; crime does not pay." If detection and conviction predominate, criminals will seek other vocations.

Technology will continue to reduce crime at an ever-increasing pace. A few simple examples—Video Cams are getting tinier and cheaper. It won't be many years until zillions of them, each with their own tiny transmitter (Have you seen the $39 Web Cams?), will be watching every inch of high-density neighborhoods. And in not too many years most of these cameras will have night vision and big brother can watch you even where there are no streetlights. Monitoring centers using Internet technology will combine functions of today's 911 centers and cops on the beat. Patrol cars can, in a few seconds, pan through every neighborhood in their precinct. But that's just the beginning, and if you're worried about big brother, get over it.

Today many people carry a cell phone. Ten years ago they were an expensive novelty. Ten years from now 'everyone' will have a cell phone that will be properly integrated with his or her home phone. People seeing a crime or accident will still call 911 as they can today. People sensing that something is amiss might dial '999.' Instantly the monitoring stations, patrol cars or whatever will zero in on the monitors watching your immediate surroundings.

Supposing that you're walking home alone on a dark and dreary night and sense that something is wrong. Somebody seems to be following you. You dial '999' and instantly the monitoring system focuses on you. They can dispatch a patrol car, if they wish; they can also call you back with instructions or queries. There's even more.

In not too many years, many of us will carry a miniature digital camera. We've discussed digital cameras in depth in an earlier chapter and, as you know, they will be no bigger than your current cell phone. It will have low light and zoom capabilities and a memory that can hold 50 high-resolution snapshots.

As you amble around town you will take pictures at the slightest provocation; after all it costs you nothing. You might take pictures at an accident or crime scene that may prove to be of value. If subsequently the police are searching for 'perps,' you can eMail them pictures that might help. It still costs you nothing.

EZ Pass systems that automatically charge your credit card for bridge tolls, etc. are just coming into their own. In not too many years automobile ID readers will be everywhere. You won't get far if you have a bunch of unpaid citations, unpaid child support of whatever. This is hardly violent crime. But how about auto theft? EZ Pass systems can identify missing autos, which will help, but there is, additionally, even better technology. Today's 'lo-jack' will in a few years be automatically installed in every car. Much like satellite tracking systems, they are now appearing in luxury cars to help you find your destination when you're lost in strange territory. These systems will instantly notify police and tell them your car's location when an unauthorized driver is hurrying toward the nearest 'chop shop.'

Crime fighting technology is rapidly approaching critical mass and crime statistics will continue to erode during the next half century. Lower crime has a positive economic impact and certainly a quality of life contribution.

High tech crime fighting will come first to major cities and any area of high-density population for obvious economic reasons. Can you accept the possibility that big, ugly cities will become demonstrably safer than small town America in the next few decades?

The Prospects for Commerce in the 21ˢᵗ Century

The prospects for commerce in the 21ˢᵗ century are wondrous to behold. Every country, even intransigent North Korea, is eager to participate in the economic sweepstakes. And if they have to blackmail their way into the game, so be it. People everywhere are clamoring for the goods and services and glamour of America. They want to sell us a lot of things cheaper than we now pay, and buy from us (for a little less) a piece of the American dream.

If the ghost of Smott-Hawley doesn't bedevil us, our global trade will grow as trade barriers fall. War, the ultimate trade barrier, is virtually outlawed. Conventional wisdom suggests that our global commerce will gradually grow as the world struggles to accommodate a market economy and participate in the largesse. This alone may be enough to justify our contention that growing commerce will contribute significantly toward 2001-2050 surpassing 1950-2000. But we feel it will be better than that; the changing nature of our commerce and the participation of emerging and re-emerging nations will be so significant that the next century will far surpass the last.

Let's examine motion pictures as an example, or better yet, a metaphor for American commerce. We are learning to produce movies with wide appeal (i.e. lots of special effects and exploding helicopters) for about $100 million. We get our money back in domestic first run and make a bundle in foreign exhibits and the cable and video after markets. That's why salaries of stars who can 'open' a picture around the world have jumped in recent years to $20 million or more.

Hollywood is beginning to realize the opportunity is huge. Its called leverage. George Lucas is going to take home half a billion from 'Star Wars 3,' much of it from overseas. Can you cope with the thought that someday soon some star (Jim Carrey?) will glean $500 million from his share of the gross from some movie that delights everyone, everywhere? As an aside, we love to hate movie stars for taking millions for what seems a few weeks work. We think the same when sport stars sign $100 million contracts. Our ire is somewhat justified with sports stars. When they sign those mammoth contracts, the price you pay for a seat skyrockets. Moreover, the rich cities pay the biggest bucks and screw up the whole league (how can anyone cheer for the Yankees? It's like cheering for Microsoft). When movie stars get zillions, you do not pay a dime more at the box office. So if the star who made a movie 'work' shouldn't get all that money, who should? Perhaps the studio bosses, the movie moguls, the corporate 'suits'? After all, we like to think some movie stars are nice people. But can you imagine any movie mogul being considered nice?

Meanwhile, back to our commerce discussion, our metaphoric movie is leveraging a high fixed cost, very low variable cost product across three hundred nations. When digital movies reach critical mass, movies can be distributed around the globe by satellite at a tiny cost compared to shipping those Brobdingnagian film cans that can cost $1000 a reel. We own less than 3% of the eyeballs. Think of the potential!

How do you measure the productivity of a fixed cost product that suddenly produces five times the revenue with no change in the manufacturing process? You can't. That's why movies are an apt metaphor for American global commerce. Television is another product with similar characteristics. I've seen every significant television broadcasting system in the world. They all seem stuck back in the '60's.

Foreign TV networks are hungry for 'product.' Product manufactured in the USA. Here again, high fixed costs (and risks) to produce the original. But the extra 200 copies of 'X-Files' for worldwide distribution cost almost nothing, yet produce millions in revenue. Do you think it costs Bill Gates much to produce another million copies of Windows for the burgeoning African market? America writes software, no one else does to any degree. Software is probably the most significant factor in the growing American domination of world commerce. And it's all (mostly) in English. It augments the case for English as truly the universal language.

All of these products involve huge initial capital, very high risk but wondrous rewards when it works. That's what America is all about: big capital, big risk, big payoff. Is anyone else doing that? And the payoff has been big and should get bigger yet. Because it all revolves around technology and we own most of that, too. Innovation, Information and Capital are our hallmark. That's the key to 21st century commerce.

The world is hungry for our technology, our movies, TV shows, sports—(how long do you think it will be before the NBA is broadcast live around the world?)— our software of all types.

I see it everywhere I go. In Africa, the Dark Continent, the lights are slowly going on. A young man in Tanzania said to me, "Your country is 200 years old. You've done many wonderful things. Our country is twenty years old, give us a chance." I was in Zanzibar 10 years later, and noticed some positive change, albeit glacial. At least the bookstores no longer feature Marxist literature.

Argentina is a country hungry to return to the first world. A century ago it was there. The 20th century was not kind to Argentina. Populist Peronista rule was dismal, followed by an even more inept military dictatorship.

In the 80's, however, one of history's silliest wars produced, ironically, a ray of hope. The macho Argentine military decided to cement their glory by grabbing the Falkland Islands, one of the few remaining shreds of the once vaunted British Empire.

If you have seen the Falklands you might well wonder why anyone would want to acquire them, and why anyone would want to defend them against invaders. The Falklands are desolate piles of granite and guano, home to hordes of miniature Penguins and Albatross. Very few people. The islands lie just north of the Antarctic and are close to nothing. Of all the places they aren't near, Argentina is the closest. The islands have no military value, no mineral value, no apparent redeeming virtue of any kind. Except perhaps as a Mecca for the misanthropic. Port Stanley is a nice place to live only if your sole alternative is going further south.

Anyway, the Argentines made their move and the equally macho Maggie Thatcher was equal to the task. The British outfitted the QEII as a troopship (they changed the bed linen to olive drab and closed the spa) and sent several thousand troops to their beleaguered outpost. After getting slapped around a bit, the Argentines fled.

The silver lining was that the Argentinean military dictatorship was so embarrassed that they all resigned. Argentina now has a modicum of civil rule and a determination to become a major participant in the world of commerce. They are the most 'North American' of the Southern Hemisphere countries and an apt partner for the extension of NAFTA. Their present archaic system of absurdly high tariffs is slowly being scrapped and prosperity could come again to Argentina. Ultimately, all Western Hemisphere nations could band together in a rough approximation of the Euro-market to the benefit of all concerned. Argentina is attempting to quell decades of rampant inflation with a peso pegged to the U.S. dollar. Keeping the peso that steady has not been a easy task, but, thus far, they are persevering. Is this a harbinger of an "Ameri-currency" emerging sometime in the next century?

In a similar vein, trade barriers around the world are crumbling, particularly with the constant prodding of the Internet. Although the Internet is reaching critical mass, eCommerce is in its infancy. Today 'eStores' are popping up everywhere. Some of them will do fine, particularly when they provide value added beyond the novelty and a slightly lower price. It may be years before the Internet has a significant share of retail sales. But it is so competitive that it forces traditional businesses to keep prices down. Result-less inflation. Many will fail, but the Internet has the potential of changing the nature of commerce in far more dramatic fashion.

Currently many businesses suffer with very high cost of customer acquisition. Cable TV, credit cards, auto insurance, home mortgages, long distance telephone, Internet access are some that suffer the most. And, as competition increases you can soon add electricity and gas to this list.

You may not be aware, but many of these businesses spend $500 or more to acquire one new customer. If you're an Internet access provider charging $20 a month, and your fixed costs eat half of that, how long will it be before a new customer is profitable? Over four years, right? If their average customer hangs around for 10 years, all is well. But they don't and it isn't. How many bank solicitations do you get every week offering you a gold card with the amazing 2.9% interest rate for 6 months? Do you know who responds?

A. People with lousy credit.
B. People who will switch for 6 mos. and then move on to the next deal.
C. Hardly anyone else.
D. All of the above.

Yes, its 'D,' and they are easily spending $500 per customer acquisition. Why do they do this? They are on a treadmill to oblivion. They must keep this customer body count steady (or growing slowly) to retain their jobs. This is why the innately highly profitable credit card business is becoming a nightmare for most providers.

Whenever you voluntarily sign up for one of these services do you sometimes feel cheated that they didn't spend $500 capturing you, or at least giving you a piece of the cost they've avoided? Well, this might just happen. A new breed of Internet providers will emerge that band people of like demographics together and puts their business out for bid. One of the first of these innovators is iPool, an Internet start-up that I have helped during the birthing process. If you join iPool, you will provide them with information about yourself that they will use to anonymously pool you with similar people. Let us suppose you are in your 50's, have no children still on the payroll, no accidents, or speeding tickets, own no 'muscle' cars, and have an unblemished credit record. You are a perfect auto insurance prospect. Insurance companies would kill to find you. But they just don't know how to locate you. iPool may have 10,000 people out of a million members that are just like you. iPool would approach the major carriers and say, "What will you charge for a group policy for 10,000 'perfect' prospects?" Believe one old auto insurance maven, when I tell you the bidding will start at 30% off the current lowest rates and go lower still. iPool would get a small piece off the top, the insurance company gets a beautiful bunch of profitable clients most of whom will never go away, the consumer gets insurance at 50 cents on the dollar.

Another example: In Minnesota, there is probably a couple million TV sets of which less than 10,000 are watched by farmers who give a hoot about pre-emergence pesticides. Yet, every spring all the network stations endlessly run pesticide spots for the chemical companies. Is this cost effective? It must cost the pesticide companies a fortune.

Working with iPool and iPool's proprietary technology, they can arrange to have their commercials only appear on the 10,000 sets belonging to people who care about pesticides. Less than 1% of the sets would receive the spot and the chemical company pays a fraction of their previous advertising expense. The networks can sell the same time spot to dozens of market segmenting merchandisers. In a sense, the advertising 'day' could become 10 times as long as it is today. Everyone benefits: Advertisers pay less, networks sell each time spot several times, iPool gets a nice fee, and the consumer get free cable for agreeing to be segmented. A complete win-win. This is what productivity is all about and another reason why 20th century prosperity past will pale beside 21st century prosperity to come.

Controlling the Economy

Perhaps the key question concerning the economy in the 21st Century is simply, "Have we learned to control the economy?" Surely the work of Fed chiefs Volker and, more recently, Greenspan, suggests we know how to rein in a rapidly expanding economy and thwart the growth of inflation. There is some evidence that we can arrest a decline and nurture an expansion as we did after the last real estate induced recession of the late 80's and when we choked off inflation during the recovery in 1991. Moreover, the work of Treasury Secretary Rubin in the bond market at the beginning of the Clinton reign stands as one of the highlights of that administration. I don't truly understand it, but am told it was a remarkable accomplishment.

We can, furthermore, point out that inventories, long the bugaboo of consistent economic performance, have been so totally harnessed by computers in this information age that overproduction and under reaction are no longer significant problems. Today a major multinational corporation with literally thousands of sales people around the world can receive daily, through the Internet, a complete rundown on all sales and near term prospects. There is no longer any excuse for missing changes in the marketplace.

Real estate is one area where, unfortunately, we haven't learned to control inventory. The Savings & Loan and the limited partnership real estate disasters caused, to a considerable degree, the two significant dips in the economy over the past twenty years. In both cases too much money was chasing too few good deals. Valuations went sky high, builders ran amok, and eventually the balloon burst, dragging the economy down with it. Gradually excess capacity is absorbed, a few monstrosities are bulldozed and the cycle starts over.

The current real estate boom seems somewhat of an anomaly; there is neither significant inflation nor any evidence of rampant overbuilding. Maybe we are learning. When Mr. Greenspan 'jawbones' about the dangers of inflation, citing that the 'savings rate' is down (which he knows is nonsense), it is because he can't very well say, "my gut tells me." When he gets the statistics he needs, managing the economy will be even more a science than an art. Are we at the point where the economy is truly under control? I'd guess we're not quite there but don't you think it might happen during the next half century?

The National Debt,
Gov't Bonds & Charity In The 21ˢᵗ Century

If you accept the premise that the next 25 years should be as good, or perhaps a tad better than the past 25 years; then I have an interesting scenario for you.

Bill Gates and Warren Buffet, two of the richest people in the world are currently worth more than 100 billion dollars. Will they continue to augment their wealth during the next 25 years at the same rate as the last 25? Hardly. But it shouldn't be too much to ask for them to perform at least at the average of all equities over the next quarter century.

Let's assume they grow a scosch better than average, say 18%, and of course, we've pegged future inflation at 3%. Now we know that Bill and Warren are big buddies. They play bridge together on the Internet and have vacationed together, riding the Trans-Siberia railroad just for fun. (It's an orient express, but far from the Orient Express).

We can also hypothesize that they will agree to pool their assets in a charitable foundation. Sure, they'll keep a billion or two out for pocket change, but the balance (about 100 billion) would be set up in a trust (both are in the process of doing so) to benefit mankind.

Where will the Bill/Warren fund be in the year 2025? Worth about $5.5 **trillion**. Enough to pay off the national debt! The ultimate charity. The debt is currently about $3 trillion, and is being monetized at the rate of 3% a year. That is, in 24 years it will have only half the impact on the GDP that it has today. Yet it seems unlikely that our august leaders will balance the budget every year for the next quarter century. We are predicting prosperity, we are not prophesying miracles. But if we have the kind of prosperity that I foresee, budget surpluses will be the norm. The politicians are already talking about paying off the debt over the next 20 years. Why bother? There's better ways to use the surplus, and besides, by 2025 the Bill/Warren fund could pay off the total debt.

Such a thought is, of course, preposterous. You can't simply write a humongous check to pay off the debt. Millions of citizens and institutions own the government bonds that comprise the debt and they might be a bit nonplussed to find their savings instruments suddenly 'called' for redemption.

Surely Government Bonds are not callable. People demand them for 'safe' investments. How would financial institutions show fiscal responsibility? By buying bonds of foreign governments?

Of course, there would be no auctions of new Treasury issues. I dare say traders in Government Bonds would be an endangered species and I've no idea how the benchmark interest rates (upon which the fixed income world relies) would be set.

A positive by-product of the great pay-off would be the elimination of U.S. Government Savings Bonds. For more than 50 years we've been implored to have a portion of our salaries set aside (the Payroll Savings Plan) to buy savings bonds. During the great war, my paper route profits bought Savings Stamps @ 10 cents which I assiduously pasted in a little book which when full, would be turned in for a $25 bond. Of course, I summarily lost the little stamp book. This patriotic effort resulted in the harried worker's painfully squirreled capital maintaining, at best, its value—that is, not earning a negative real rate of return. There was many a year (during the 70's and early 80's) where the inflation rate was higher than the return on these pitiful instruments. I have no recollection of any Treasury official, economic consultant or pure economist from academia ever denigrating these instruments for what they are—an extremely poor way to accumulate capital for long term needs. Since they had ten-year maturities, surely they were designed for long term needs.

Savings accounts with minuscule interest rates can be justified for short-term savings for a specific purpose—a vacation, a new car, etc. Yet millions of hard working Americans sacrificed mightily to put their money in savings bonds to pay their children's college tuition some 20 years later. In 1960 $1000 would buy a year's tuition at many a fine institution of higher learning. Put into savings bonds and years later, with all its accrued interest, it wouldn't buy a semester's tuition at some of these same institutions.

I was as oblivious as anyone about negative investing until one day nearly 20 years ago I asked our human resources director why our company did nothing to promote the Payroll Savings Plan. "Not on my watch," was the reply, "savings bonds are a cruel hoax." After considerable questioning and investigation I realized that he was absolutely right and found myself admiring a personnel executive. Something I never thought would happen to me.

We had some savings bonds—about eight of them, with a total face value of $250. My parents, back in the sixties, were given to giving bonds in fits and starts to commemorate holidays, grandchildren's birthdays etc, and teach us the value of frugality. The bonds cost them about $200 and were all gifts on various occasions between 1968-1971.

I recently cashed them in. The bank gave me $1100. Hardly a windfall. Just suppose that I cashed them in back in 1971 and put the proceeds (e.g. $200) in any one of the top five mutual of that time (there weren't that many to choose from). If I kept it intact until now, I could cash it in for a 'Cherokee,' or 'Trooper' or another of those neat SUV trucks that costs $25,000 or more! I can get a super bicycle for $1100.

Of course, Bill and Warren won't pay off the debt and we'll still be extolled to buy bonds. All I want to do is plant a seed in your mind. When they say 'Buy Bonds,' you say, "Why on earth would I do that?" Yet, sadly enough, 45 million Americans own savings bonds. Because they're 'safe.' Safe from what? Safe from any reasonable gain?

Savings Bonds are but a minor example of anachronistic government policy. Social Security (so counter productive that we'll call it Social InSecurity) is the ultimate in well intentioned but terribly misguided government policy. Even more troubling is that many who claim they want to reform Social InSecurity fail to see the fundamental inefficiency of the old age assistance program. Even the idea of investing some of the Social Security Administration's trust fund in equities is misbegotten. It would only serve to forestall the ultimate bankruptcy of Social InSecurity. Even if the program were actuarial sound (which it can never be) it would not be an effective way to help the working poor achieve a dignified old age.

There are several other examples of government policy and tradition that misguide us, and lead us to accept unacceptable government policies and practices. We will explore the anachronistic 'savings rate' a measure so absurd that we often refer to it as the 'frugaling rate.' We are a nation that measures its 'growth' with a factor called 'productivity.' Productivity went nowhere for most of the last half century, we were told over and over, averaging only a dreary 1% a year until the last few years. Yet, during much of that time, the wealth held by our fellow Americans grew by leaps and bounds. It didn't take a Baker scholar to see that something was amiss. Recently economists admitted that maybe there was something wrong with the productively measure. Maybe an industrial productivity measure has less relevance in a nation whose economy is only 20% industrial. Maybe even that number is suspect, since 'outsourcing' is counted in the service economy, even though it usually involves manufacturing.

The real culprit in all of this is probably our beloved government. Most statistical 'rates'—savings, dividend, productivity, trade—were devised in a century gone by and many of the factors are no longer relevant. Rather than spend money on new, relevant measures, our government continues to spend millions on inappropriate measures that the financial press and the public review and worry about. It appears that the only 'statistics' that you can rely on are opinion polls, like the Conference Board's Consumer Confidence survey, that accurately reports attitudes.

Another dire measurement that never seems to make any difference is the balance of payments. It seems to me we've always been in a hole and it seems like it's always getting worse. I think I understand that when we buy a lot more goods from foreign countries than we sell them in return, it can cheapen our currency which makes their goods more expensive, which causes inflation, swollen glands and a lot of verbal diarrhea from economic observers. But doesn't it seem that nothing much ever really happens? Perhaps the problem is that the 'trade deficit' is a 1950's phenomenon when there were nation-states (but not any more) and there was no global economy (there is now). The numbers are inaccurate and irrelevant, except it costs more to travel abroad.

Maybe we should have measures that gauge the influx of capital from around the world and the impact of that capital as it is leveraged in myriad new ventures. As a matter of fact, non-Americans do own a substantial portion of our equities. But, of course, we reciprocate by purchasing significant quantities of foreign securities particularly now that emerging markets are back in favor. They may well offset each other.

But here's an interesting thought. The balance of payments has been chronically poor, and now worse than ever—some 10-15 billion dollars each month, and there's a lot of hand wringing when the numbers are announced. How's this for coincidence? For the last four or five year foreigners have increased their ownership of U.S. treasury bonds by about 10-15 billion dollars, net, each month. It looks like all the excess of exports over imports is going right into importing treasuries. Foreigners now own 40% of our national debt. In Japan (where much of the trade deficit occurs) government bonds pay a magnificent 1.5%. If they can quadruple their take with U.S. treasuries then they have benefited from our 'goods and services.' If the trade deficit continues as it has the last few years it is not really a deficit at all, and it might actually be in our best interest. Americans are learning that treasuries are horrible long term investments and if no one else buys them the price will go down, and the interest rate, up. We don't want that.

It's interesting to note that foreign investors are willing to take the exchange rate risk in acquiring U.S. treasuries. They must feel that our economy will remain strong, we'll have budget surpluses, and when the bonds mature, they won't take a significant exchange rate hit. Incidentally, if a Japanese citizen buys a U.S. treasury, which pays 6%, and Japan has no inflation, what is his real rate of return? Anyway, when you hear the trade deficit numbers you will not be depressed, you'll be elated that someone has the money to shop at our 'bond store.' Maybe we could persuade Japanese firms to offer our savings bonds through payroll savings.

Maybe its time to redefine the USA. When we say America is no longer an industrial economy but a service economy, one gets the picture that all the new jobs are at McDonalds. What we really are is an innovation nation, with millions of eager young entrepreneurs willing to gamble it all on a new technology, Internet gimmick, wonder drug, software, or what have you. It's a country where every person can become a venture capitalist, eager to pour money in these ventures. We have not yet come to grips with what we are and what we are doing. As the tentacles of the Internet encircle the globe, a host of givens will be gone, trade barriers will tumble, and the rules of the game will change.

Today we dominate the world militarily. We dominate capital markets and are the world's hard currency of choice. We dominate in technological development and innovation. Ours is the universal language. Tomorrow we may dominate the world's economy. Maybe we do already.

If all this is so, perhaps productivity, balance of payments, unemployment statistics, savings rates and a lot of other sacred cows may not be as sacred as the cows become dogs. In a few years we'll have the world's first trillionaire and Bill Gates will probably say "well, OK, but a trillion ain't what it used to be."

And if the Bill and Warren trillions don't go to paying off the national debt, what will happen to the money? They could easily disgorge $200 billion or so each year in the name of charity. We can hope they'll find a better vision than the software executive who gave $200 million to aid stray cats.

There is so much happening that has no precedent that I personally feel prosperity in the next fifty years will exceed our wildest imagination. The potential of the next half-century fair boggles the mind. But all I ask is that you accept a premise that 2000-2049 will be a tad better than 1950-1999. Maybe prosperity is reaching its critical mass. Anyway, we're determined to help you think of your long term investment decisions in terms of the future, not of the past.

III. Planning for Retirement

Saving Vs. Investing

Economics pundits often write gloomy articles on the sorry state of the savings rate in the United States. The savings rate is often cited as an example of American profligacy that will have dire consequences in inevitable rampant inflation and economic catastrophe. Said writers habitually make invidious comparisons of our frugality with that of the Japanese, a thrifty folk who are accustomed to 'saving' 6-8% of their income. These comparisons are less evident since the Japanese economy went down the drain. Meanwhile our savings rate approaches zero with much accompanying hand wringing by the experts.

Just what is the 'savings rate,' and how important is it? In calculating the savings rate the government attempts (and fails) to calculate the difference between personal income and personal expense with the residue being the savings component. The savings rate essentially becomes the net inflows of time deposits into the U.S. banking system. This does not include ordinary checking accounts; which are demand deposits. The bank must give you your money when you demand it (i.e. present a check, ATM, or debit card). Time deposits are those that a bank can refuse to give you until some time after you demand it (usually 30 days). This was a useful distinction during the early years of the great depression when there was an abiding fear of 'runs' on the bank when rumors of insolvency incited depositors to run to the bank and demand their money. Often the rumor became a self-fulfilling prophecy.

Banks rarely, if ever, refuse to honor any request for funds, time deposit rules not withstanding. But they will often extract "a substantial penalty for early withdrawal" and take back much of the miserable interest your deposit has earned.

'Pass-book' savings (or whatever the bank calls them, since no one has pass books any more) and certificates of deposit (CD's) of varying maturities and MMA's (Money Market Accounts) are the primary examples of time deposits. Since one presumes this money is being put away for a 'rainy day' it contributes to the 'saving rate' that has long been used as a measure of American frugality. Demand deposits (your checking account) are considered to be your 'cash on hand' and are hardly savings for the future, rainy or not. Of course, many people keep enormous sums in checking accounts because they are too rich, lazy, or uninformed to manage it properly.

That isn't all. Many folks put their cash reserve in a checking account that pays interest. This is called a NOW account and is technically a time deposit and consequently gets counted in the 'savings rate.' We keep our cash in NOW accounts since at least we get 1% interest for leaving more cash in these accounts than we probably should. My wife, Anita has an abiding distaste for being overdrawn, and considering my casual altitude toward record keeping her apprehension is well founded. Nonetheless these NOW accounts are our day-to-day checking accounts and are by no stretch of the imagination qualify as savings. I suspect many others do the same.

Despite all the hand wringing, the fact that the 'savings rate' has declined to near zero is actually a wonderful thing. It means that people aren't banking on the banks for long term investing. Does it mean they aren't saving for their golden years?

Quite the contrary. It means that people may finally be waking up and are saving for retirement in an effective and relevant manner. Are consumers consuming all their disposable income? If so, then where are the zillions of dollars of net inflows into the mutual funds coming from? The 'savings rate' can't measure these dollars. They look like expenses. Nor can it measure any kind of equity investing as savings.

Years ago, it dawned on the general public that 'saving' through purchasing whole life insurance was not a really good idea. Yet Life Insurance companies were the number one repository for consumer savings as recently as 1950. They are no longer relevant. The banks are soon to follow.

My local bank in Manhattan has a sign in the window that says, "Can You Retire on Social Security?" Beneath are the words "check savings." The implication is that you can enhance your post 65 quality of life with regular saving through your checking account. Let's test this hypothesis and see what happens. Let's suppose, Mr. Benny, that you are 39, living close to the financial edge, and are beginning to worry about retirement. You know that Social InSecurity will pay you about $10-13,000 (constant dollars) when you're 65 (for some it's 67) And you've been putting as much as you can into a 401K. You've been told that your 401K, along with Social InSecurity, will allow you to live medium (it would take a lot more to live large) for about the first 10 years of retirement. That's assuming that you believe $30,000 a year will provide you with a comfortable retirement in the community of your choice. Let's hope you don't choose Manhattan.

If you've read current anti-aging information carefully you know that lacking any obvious genetic defects, you're on track to live to be 100 or more. So you'd better do something to supplement your meager Social InSecurity pay out for the final 25 years or so after your 401K runs out at age 75.

After excruciating budgetary analysis (although budgets work only for the most anal of us) you determine that you can eke out about $1000 a year to save for these later golden years. Being a cautious and frugal person you decide to save the money through your checking account into a companion savings account. You'll put $1000 each year into a Roth IRA (to keep it tax-free) identified with the projected year of withdrawal. Thus the first $1000 (this year) will be labeled Roth 2035 (your 75th year), next year you'll put $1000 into a new Roth IRA called 2036 (your 76th year) and so on.

So, after 36 years, how much will you add to your Social InSecurity income in current dollars? Well, you'll draw about 4% interest on your savings account. And we'll say inflation will only be about 2% (which of course is optimistic, since recent history suggests that 3% would be a more honest estimate). But we'll give the bank the benefit of the doubt, making our real return 4%—2% inflation, or 2% net. Your painfully saved $1000 will have, 36 years hence, the buying power of $2,000. Add this to your Social InSecurity and you'll live on the magnificent sum of $15,000 annually. Your cup runneth under.

"Aha," you say, "no-one is dumb enough to put money in a passbook type savings account for 36 years." Although it is arguable, we'll concede the point. You'll put your money in 10 year CD's or 30-year treasuries or whatever. And we'll give you 6% interest (which is high), subtract out 2% inflation (which is low) giving you a very bank biased 4% real interest. You know by now that your $1000 will double every 18 years at 4% interest, so your additional income at age 75 will be $4,000. Add that to your Social InSecurity of $13,000 and you'll receive from ages 75–100 an annual income of $17,000. You will eat, unfortunately, very low on the hog.

If we agreed that the first half of the new century (2001-2050) will be at least a bit better than the previous half century (1951-2000), would it not be adequately conservative to project that we can achieve the same investment returns that have been realized over the past 25 years? Not better, mind you, just equal.

To begin with, inflation has averaged 5% over the last 25 years. This, of course, is badly distorted by those dreadful early years (despite the impact of those WIN-Whip Inflation Now!—buttons) and we know the past 10 years has produced a more rational 3% inflation. But we'll live with our 'givens;' we wouldn't want anyone to think that we're 'limboughing' the numbers.

Rather than put the money in the bank (where, it may not grow at all, and even if it does, we'll get negligible impact) we'll try the stock market. Our returns will be with 95% certainty (as the scientists always say, but it doesn't mean much) approximately the following:

A. Choose a S&P index fund—No thinking required here, we'll just tag along with the market—12% annual returns in constant dollars, or

B. Pick a good, solid growth mutual fund—perhaps not top 10 over the past 25 years, but well into the top 20. We used IDS Growth Fund as our example. Fifteen percent net annual return. Finally, for the risk prone,

C. Select a top ranked fund with a touch of market timing—if you pick a front runner and exercise a modicum of market timing (which we'll explain later), you might achieve a long-term return of 18%. We can't give this one a 95% probability—who knows what you can hope for?

So what happens to the $1000 we so carefully squirrel away each year for the wonder years after 75? Let's look at all our options:

Vehicle	Net Interest Rate	Constant $'s	Probability of Success
		(Pay out in 36 Yrs.)	
Savings Bank	2%	$ 2,000	99.9%
10 Yr. CD's-			
30 Yr. Treasuries	4%	$ 4,000	99.9%
S & P Index Fund	12%	$ 64,000	95.0%
Growth Fund	15%	$ 190,000	95.0%
'Super' Fund/timing	18%	$ 512,000	??%

There are your choices. Which retirement plan is best for you? If it isn't obvious to you, maybe you don't deserve to be saved, but maybe I can further alleviate your fears. What is the consequence of achieving the 5% risk of 'failure' in our mutual fund examples? What's the worst that can happen?

Conventional thinking suggests that the market might tank the week before you make your first retirement fund redemption. Let's say it drops 50% overnight. The worst such disaster in modern history was the October '87 thud. Most mutual funds lost 20-30% of their value almost overnight. By the following spring the market had regained all its losses and then some. So if we concede a 50% thumping the next question is, how long does the pain last? The most likely scenario is that the market will recover in a year or less. If you invested in a growth fund and were expecting a check for $190,000, you'd get one for $95,000 (still substantially better than $4,000, don't you think?) And if the market returned to 'par' in a year but never really compensated for the sudden drop, your pay out in future years will have lost one year's compounding—or 15%. In following years you'll redeem each year mutual funds worth about $160,000 (constant dollars), about 15% lower than the $190,000 you expected. How does that look versus $4,000?

Actually a worse scenario might be if the market tanked early in your years of enlightened investing. Let's suppose the market dropped 50% in your fifth investing year and didn't recover for 11 years! This is about as long as the great depression of 1929-1940. The recession of '74 was also pretty grim. But is this now beyond the realm of possibility? Quite likely. But let's go with it and see what happens. The portfolios you set up over the first five years are, at year 16, right where they were at year 5. They have only 20 years to go before they start maturing, so they can't end up at the point you hoped they'd be when you set them up. The simple answer is that they will miss two 'turns' (e.g. they double every 4.8 years at 15% compound annually). Consequently, they will not double twice during the monster recession of 2005-15. The S&P 500 gained nothing (net of inflation) in the 1973—1983 troubles. Please note, however, that 'good' mutual funds returned 2—4%, compound, over that time.

Five 'turns' instead of seven means that during the first five years of your second stage retirement (remember that years 65-75 were covered by Social InSecurity plus your modest 401K retirement program), you'll receive 'only' $32,000 each year to supplement your Social InSecurity. How does that compare with your very safe bank producing $2-4,000 a year?

But there's more. We've established that over 50 years, the average return on a 'good' mutual fund will equal that of the last quarter of the 20th century. About 15% net compound growth, as I recall. But our initial investments have, after 16 years, barely doubled. Work it through to make sure you understand. The $1000 invested in year one, doubles by year five (15% compounding) then crashes back to $1,000 in year six and has struggled back to $2,000 by year 16. Doubling in 16 years means average compound interest of 4.5%. (Rule of 72: 72 divided by 16=4.5). If our growth rate is 4.5% over the first 16 years and will prove to be 15% after 50 years, it must go 'blue blazes' during years 17-50.

It's easy enough to figure out. If the average rate for years 17-50 is 18%, net of inflation our money will double every 4 years. Thus, near the end of the half century (in '48) our little fund will be worth over $500,000. Actually the market needs to grow at a little over 19% per year to reach our 50 year average of 15%. Although going nowhere after 16 years (even then it's better than a 'savings bank'), a modest increase in the projected average rate over the later years provides huge returns. Behold the power of 'time value of money'! You have to make choices: invest and be secure with securities, save and be left behind.

Skeptics who can't stomach the idea of investing totally in equities raise the one doomsday example that might spell misery to the equity investor. They cite Morton Gottbucks who retired in 1968 with a $500,000 kitty, all invested in S & P index funds. In 1973 the market tanks, loses 40%. Ten years later the S & P index had grown 8.2%, inflation was up 8.1% and Gottbucks was dead in the water (although I suspect he made a bundle on his home). If a big piece of his half million were in corporate bonds he wouldn't be broke by '93; he'd hang on quite a few more years. Scary, isn't it? But let's look at some reasons why our approach—stay with equities makes a lot of sense.

I.   Could this happen again? Probably not. In 1973 we had just lost a very dumb war; so dumb that we didn't dare raise taxes to pay for it. We followed that with 10 years of really dumb economic policy (WIN buttons) and a really dumb Fed. We're smarter than that now. Could something else, equally drastic, happen? Sure it could. What is the likelihood? Much less in the 21st Century.

2.   We never advocate investing in hot stocks. We always advocate well-respected growth mutual funds, rather than the S & P 500 index. There is a huge difference between 15% and 12%. The better funds (not necessarily the best) during the 1973-83 decade returned 4.7% annually. Gottbucks' plan called for 7% net annual growth in his portfolio. If he followed our advice he'd have his money in mutual funds that would be close to meeting his original plan.

3.   Our philosophies call for making, each year, new investment portfolios for the distant future, say 30 years. In Gottbucks case he should put away (in tax free Roth IRA's-his wife's still working) $2,000, a year. This accomplishes a form of dollar cost averaging. In '73 after the crash, Gottbuck's $2,000 bought the fund at a 40% discount. That portfolio and those of the years following should grow at a faster rate than our 12% average over 50 years. Helpful hint: If you're setting up a new portfolio each year, have your money ready (borrow it if you must) to invest at the bottom of a correction. We seem to have a correction (or two) most every year. If the market booms during the first half of the year, there's a good chance there will be a correction (i.e. a 10% drop) before yearend. This pattern is somewhat typical, it seems money managers try extra hard during the winter and

if successful, get more conservative during the summer and the market gives back some of the gains. Your CNBC experts will tell you when there is a correction, and tell you again with it appears over.

4.   If none of this assuages your fears, I will make one concession. If you have set up portfolios for each year of retirement, rather than one pile of money, you can maintain control without losing your perspective. To avoid the anxiety of anticipating a market crash as you near your retirement date you might consider the following:

About 6 years (but no longer) before your retirement date convert your first retirement year portfolio to bonds. If today were that day, you would convert your 2006 portfolio to a mixture of bonds. Frankly, I would go for high yield bond funds, AKA Junk Bonds. Junk bonds were excoriated in the '80's but have proved to be very stable and satisfying investments. You might put a chunk into a well-regarded corporate bond fund. You might put some in government bonds, so if you're so compelled go ahead and do it, you wimp!

The mix we suggest should produce returns in the 8-9% area, not the doubling you planned for that portfolio over the final six years, but a reasonable and rather predictable return, nonetheless. Each year you will convert the next sequential portfolio of retirement funds. In our example, in the year 2001 you would convert the 2007 portfolio, in 2002, the 2008 portfolio, and so on.

One final thought, if the market has been 'boppin' alone in high gear and the portfolio is ahead of scheduled growth, you might well be advised to lock in the gains by converting it to bonds, maybe even seven years out. Conversely, if the market has been sluggish for awhile and you think the country is coming out of a mild recession you might opt to ride it out without ever converting a given year's portfolio. In any event a little rational thought and sober planning, rather than emotional, knee-jerk reaction, will go far in keeping your retirement portfolio safe from the vicissitudes of short-term economic fluctuations.

No Credit for Debit Cards

While we are in the process of castigating banks, let's discuss credit cards and particularly debit cards. I can't relate to debit cards. We spent our youth playing the float, passing checks on the weekend and praying that my paycheck would be deposited on Tuesday before the checks cleared. In the halcyon days of high interest rates one could make a buck or two by carefully playing the float. I guess this is neither relevant nor possible anymore.

Debit cards are a great deal for the banks. They get their full discount from the merchant and carry no loss reserves. There is no chance they will not get paid. The merchants are the ones getting hosed. But it's no big deal for you either. Float isn't, of course, much of a factor. Thirty days float on $1000 in a NOW account is about $1.

Much more important is the lost opportunity cost by using a debit card. Do you collect 'frequent flyer' miles? If you don't collect them, hate travel and dislike vacations of any kind, skip to the next section. Otherwise, read on.

The trend toward 'unexpirable' miles is a good one. American Express has always done so. The big carriers are following the lead of Northwest/Continental and making their miles last forever. Some airlines require that you fly on a paid ticket occasionally, but all in all, the trend is positive.

If you are organized enough to use a debit card without being chronically overdrawn, the following should work for you. To begin with, mileage can be a lot more valuable than most critics are willing to admit. They peg the value at $200-300 per 25,000 miles (the amount generally required to earn a free ticket) because a super-saver tourist ticket can often be acquired at that price. Anyone who uses mileage in lieu of buying a deep discount ticket is a prime candidate for the 'dumb and dumber' club.

We have traveled extensively and over the past 15 years, accumulated (and used) over 5 million miles (or points) with Northwest Airlines (how else do you get out of Minneapolis in the winter?), American Express and Marriott Hotels. Right now, we have about a million miles in our various accounts. We have never used airline miles unless we were sure we were getting $1000 or more value for each 25,000 miles cashed in.

An obvious example is to use mileage for long domestic trips where you can't stay over Saturday night. That ticket will cost you $600-$1500 otherwise. An even better example is international travel. We have often flown to the Orient and oftentimes bargain tickets can be found for $500—$800. But a 15-hour flight in coach is a discomfort I refuse to experience in my dotage. Business class tickets run $3500—$5000 and are seldom discounted (except perhaps for the Amex Platinum's buy one, get one free). The simple solution is to buy a $500 bargain ticket to Hong Kong and upgrade it with 50,000 miles. Since you're traveling 10,000 miles or more each way, you'll earn 20,000+ miles, so your total cost is $500 plus 30,000 miles, instead of $3,500 or more for a ticket up front.

If you are satisfied that mileage is valuable, the answer to debit cards is to acquire an American Express Card and/or a Visa sponsored by your favorite airline. You can then execute a bank authorization permitting them to automatically deduct the total monthly bill from your checking account on the last day of the grace period. It will work just like a debit card. Instead of deducting from your checking account each time you go to the market, it saves them up and debits your checking account a month later. The float will help pay for the card(s) and, of course, you earn mileage every time you shop. If you absolutely refuse to ever use cash, you can build up a respectable balance even if you do not fly much (if at all). Your reward is then a nice free vacation every few years plus the knowledge that the credit card issuer is making very little money from you since you never pay any credit card interest.

Prosperity, P/E's and the Press

We are living in a time of unprecedented prosperity. The United States is king of the hill. Everyone who wants a job can find one, maybe not quite what they want, where they want, but work is plentiful. We have not had a whiff of recession for nearly ten years and confidence is high. Much of the rest of the world is struggling out of recession. Their troubles bothered us not a whit, despite the collapse of the second strongest economy in the world and the subsequent ripples that engulfed much of Southeast Asia. That giant sucking sound is not jobs going south, but Ross Perot gasping for breath as NAFTA dazzles.

The financial press has been predicting the imminent demise of the bull market for the past five years. The economists generally agree. We all know that prosperity can't go on forever (It can't?). The stock market aptly reflects this prosperity as well as enthusiasm for the future. The current market P/E (price-earning ratio) is a stratospheric, by historical standards, 27. The DOW P/E, however, remains a relatively benign 22.

A recent *Fortune* retirement article pointed out that historically, market P/E's over 20 were soon followed by a decade of dreadfully slow growth. Is this relevant? It's hardly a good omen. I can remember that at the height of the Japanese boom, one observer opined that their current P/E of 50 was OK for Japan. After all they were different from the U.S. Wrong. Real estate speculation and cartel management practices fueled Japanese prosperity. Both ultimately had to pay the piper.

If investors place a 27 P/E on the U.S. stock market it is simply a reflection of the present value they place on the individual companies' future prospects. Hot stocks in new industries command P/E's in the hundreds, if not infinity. Unbridled enthusiasm and wild speculation? Perhaps. Many of these companies will falter, some will fail, but some will make it, big time.

Dull, good old boy companies don't have huge P/E's. Big auto has a most modest P/E and so perceptively so. They'll probably never regain their primacy past. *Fortune* ridicules one author who purportedly feels that the Dow will hit 36,000 and P/E's will reach 100, stocks being terribly undervalued, in his opinion. A 36,000 Dow is no big deal. Near 12,000 now, it will triple in about 9 years with 12% annual growth. Most Dow companies build their annual plans around 10-15% growth, unless there are extenuating circumstances. If they do grow 10% a year, pretty much on plan, the Dow will surely grow 12% a year.

Stocks go up when earnings go up. But this no longer has much to do with dividends. Dividends are taxable as ordinary income and corporate executives do not increase dividends because their pay is not tied to dividend pay out. Growth in stocks retained over a year is taxed as capital gains, better for all shareholders, especially corporate executives. Executive pay is more and more being tied to stock performance. Makes sense. CEO's don't want big salaries, or even big bonuses. They want big options to make the really big bucks if the stock shoots skyward. Many such firms pay nothing, or a tiny fraction of their earnings as dividends. These firms often spend big chunks of their earnings on stock buyback plans, which effectively reduce the number of publicly held shares and thus automatically raises the earnings per share. A company that buys back 2% of its stock each year will increase its earnings per share 2% a year even if its basic business only breaks even. Thus, if you can raise your earnings from operations by 10% a year and reduced your stock outstanding by 2% a year, your company will show steady earnings growth of 12% a year and it will be well regarded on Wall St. The stock price will probably go up faster than 12% a year and therefore its P/E ratio will get higher and higher.

One of the traditional benchmarks of stock market values is the 'dividend rate.' The theory is that if stock prices go up and dividends don't rise the investor is getting a smaller return on their investment and consequently the stocks are overpriced vis á vis the returns on other financial instruments.

This was all very relevant when widows and orphans lived off their AT&T dividends, but that quaint notion belongs to a time gone by. These days the stock paying the highest dividend rate (excluding utility stocks, which are really bonds in disguise) is likely to be one whose stock price has collapsed (see 'dogs of the Dow'). More significantly, as we have noted, many companies are eschewing dividends in favor of stock buyback plans. Money that would ordinarily be paid to stock-holders as dividends (taxable both to the corporation and the stock-holder), is used instead to reduce the number of publicly held shares. This tends to increase the price of the stock, in effect paying a 'dividend' to the stockholder.

A substantial number of companies are electing to use increased earnings to buy back stock in lieu of granting or increasing dividends. The number of S&P 500 companies that don't pay dividends is approaching 40%, which produces a lower dividend rate. Doesn't it strike you that 'dividend rate' as a meaningful measure is becoming an anachronism much like 'savings rate,' 'prime rate,' 'trade deficit' and other outmoded and generally useless economic measures?

Since there is an ever-decreasing pool of stock available and more and more demand for stocks the prices (and the P/E's) will obviously rise. But average P/E's of 100? That sounds a bit goofy, even to me. A Dow of 36,000 and P/E's of 100 in combination is a recipe for tragedy. If the Dow hits 36,000 with P/E's at 100 it connotes rampant, out of control speculation. A tulip bulb frenzy, if you will. The Dow should hit 36,000 in ten years or less with corporate earnings increasing 10% or so a year and the P/E moving very slowly upward, if at all. If earnings grow 12% or more a year and P/E's do reach 100, the Dow will be over 136,000 not 36,000. You can do the math. Can you imagine a day when the Dow goes down 1,000 (it's never happened yet) and it's considered routine (i.e. less than 1% loss)?

If the prospects for the next century are quite good, there's nothing innately wrong with P/E's of 100 for companies with great prospects and an ever-decreasing number of shares. But, if we're living in a fool's paradise, than a dreary decade of low returns may well be in the offing.

If CEO's and their top minions are to get rich on stock options, they must perforce increase the number of shares in the public domain because exercising stock options turns treasury stock into public stock. When a company announces a stock buyback program they invariably are planning to 'restock' the treasury for future option programs as well as reduce the supply and raise the earnings per share as we've described.

If a company's employee stock option plan is properly structured, the executive group will get rich if the company does very well. Yet it amazes me how shareholders will bitch when someone like Sandy Weill draws a $100 million out of exercised options as his annual pay.

I first encountered Sandy Weill shortly after he, as President of American Express, had persuaded CEO Jimmy Robinson III to acquire my employer, IDS. It was the best acquisition 'three sticks' ever made, which isn't saying much, since most of his acquisitions were dogs. Not the least of which, ironically, was Sandy's own creation, the Shearson-Hamill brokerage firm. Sandy joined AmEx as part of that deal.

We humble mid-westerners were ecstatic about being acquired, but faced our first planning meeting with the New York contingent with some trepidation. Sandy led the insurgents and was accompanied by senior executives like Lew Gerstner, who knew all about 'S' curves from his McKinsey background and later applied this knowledge with remarkable results when he coaxed IBM into reinventing itself. Ed Cutler represented Firemen's Fund (another acquisition that barked) and Peter

Cohen, Shearson's CEO was there reluctantly and didn't hesitate to show his disdain for the acquisition. During a key 'show and tell' by our marketing chief, Peter opened up a *Wall St. Journal* and blatantly read it during the presentation. You can imagine how distraught we were several years later when the barbarians devoured Cohen at the gate.

Anyway we convened for lunch, hosted by our new but soon to be erstwhile CEO, Wally Scott. At one point Sandy asked Wally why we couldn't install a system of 'lock boxes,' which is simply a method of expediting the deposit of mutual funds shareholders' purchases into interest bearing bank accounts. In those days of double-digit interest rates, expediting the mail a day or two could mean big money. "We could," replied Wally, "but that interest belongs to the shareholders." Try to imagine Sandy's retort.

I must say that to my knowledge Sandy never did 'do' his shareholders, individually or collectively. Quite the contrary, shareholders of his empire, cobbled together from a variety of failing enterprises, schlock outfits and has-beens (all prior to the Citicorp marriage), have done very well indeed. When stockholders complain about Sandy's annual stock option windfall, they are being most disingenuous. Sandy doesn't get a big payoff unless the stockholders get a big payoff.

In any event, as more companies move toward buyback plans, the pool of available stock shrinks, stock prices and P/E's will be pushed upward. In the future a stock's price will be determined by money managers' (and to a minor extent the public's) perception of the ability of management to increase the company's stock price. A company that encourages its management to get rich if the stock goes up will be well received on Wall St. If the company can also produce steady growth in earnings it will command a higher P/E. Wall St. hates surprises, actually the street hates bad surprises. American Express had 500 million shares outstanding a few years ago, now it's about 450 million. Can you do the math?

You could do worse than to set up your own 'mutual fund' consisting of stocks from well respected companies that have liberal stock option plans, buy back strategies and are openly de-emphasizing dividends. Incidentally if real Social InSecurity reform is enacted and truly privatized pensions become a reality, the market will have to absorb as much as an additional $150 billion of new money each year. This is bound to put upward pressure on market P/E's. A market P/E of 100? Who knows? Who cares? What we do know is the present market P/E of 27, high by historical standards, is not necessarily a harbinger of disasters to come.

Prosperity and Financial Planners

It is heartening to see so many citizens turning to professionals to help them get their financial house in order and plan for retirement. It is not my intent to present a treatise on financial planning. If you are unaware of such tenets as 'dollar cost averaging,' 'pay yourself first,' etc., you should read David Chilton's wonderful easy-read little book called *The Wealthy Barber* (check your Internet booksellers).

It is disheartening to see financial planners wedded to some principals that can mislead if not discourage anyone struggling to improve their golden years. The highly mathematical analysis presented in the *Fortune* article (and I've seen many other very much like it), suggests that a 30 year old must put $10,000 into a 401K plan every year until retirement 35 years hence in order to have a 55% probability of achieving a retirement income of $100,000 a year. Social InSecurity and other savings would be a bonus. Moreover, sayeth *Fortune* if the planee were 40 and hadn't gotten started on saving for retirement, the price would be $21,000 a year for the following 25 years.

I don't know how many concerned 30 year olds have $10,000 a year to put away but I suspect they are in the minority. Clearly this analysis could cause many to become very discouraged. Why is this analysis so dramatically different from the various examples we've used throughout this text?

To begin with, we'll use age 29 instead of 30 to give us 36 years before retirement. To do all the math in our head we have to stick with powers of 2. That, of course, shouldn't make much difference. We also show results of various interest assumptions, all of which have some historical legitimacy, and leave it to the reader to decide what's most likely.

We've cited many reasons why we think the next 50 years will be at least as good as the last 25 and precious few suggesting things will get worse. Thus investing $10,000 a year at age 29 for 36 years should match up pretty well with what's happened over the past 25 years. Your choices, in descending order:

A. Top ranked Mutual Fund
    If the top 10 growth mutual funds perform as did the top ten of the late 20th century your retirement income per year (your target is $100,000) will be, at 18% annually, adjusted for inflation: $5,120,000.00
B. Stock Index Fund
    Historical Stock index (S&P 500) for the past quarter century, net at 12%: $ 640,000.00
C. Very conservative mix of stocks and bonds producing an inflation adjusted return of 8%: $ 160,000.00
D. Corporate bond fund producing net return of 6% $ 80,000.00

The huge inflation of the late 70's and early 80's severely depressed the returns in our example. Those dreadful early years made the 25 year average inflation about 5%, rather than the more realistic 3% we've enjoyed for the past decade or two. [Actually less than 3% for the past 10 years.] Do you really expect double digit inflation in the next half century?

The *Fortune* mathematicians seem to have used something between our examples (C) & (D) to arrive at their $100,000 retirement. In my experience 8% is the rate du jour across the financial services industry. Why so conservative? After all, the last decade to produce a net return less than 8% as 1978-1987. The last decade to produce such a low return among top rated mutual funds was 1974-1983. These planners are expecting perhaps an ugly war followed by horrible double-digit inflation in the next decade or two? I don't think so.

What they are expecting is to get a lot of flack if for whatever reason a client fails to achieve wondrous returns on their investing. If the planner were affiliated with a large firm, the firm's compliance department wouldn't dream of allowing any illustration that hints at larger returns. The result is that brokerage firms, independent planners and even the financial press all use 8% annual portfolio growth as a CYA strategy. If you think CYA stands for Catholic Youth Army you have problems beyond retirement planning.

It wasn't so long ago that agents of the Pru, the Met and many other big life insurance companies were, in desperate attempts to forestall an inexorably declining market, selling life products as pension products. They 'promised' (illustrated) returns that became impossible when interest rates plummeted in the late 80's. Regulators decided these companies were gulling a gullible public. Class action suits cost them a bundle. Class action suits made a bundle for many lawyers, not all of whom had the best interests of the public as their primary motivation.

So no one dares present optimistic illustrations of potential returns and all the fine mathematical projections rest on the simplifying assumption that the (financial) world is flat. But flat it is not; it has remarkable fizz and is going to bubble along indefinitely and may never really burst.

Rather than present a near hopeless plan that requires a young person take a vow of poverty now in order to live large 35 years hence, I would much rather show them how a modest amount put away at an early age can really pay off at sunset time.

Throughout this treatise I have stressed the technique of saving each year the base amount needed for a specific retirement year in the future, rather than dumping all your money into one big pot that someday might produce a reasonable return each year over a given number of years. Realistically, we often have no choice, (such as with a 401K) but to follow the big pot approach even though it requires an actuary steeped in regression analysis to show how you're going to do many years hence. I'd much rather set up new Roth IRA for each retirement year after a predetermined interval. To a 30-year-old that doesn't have $10,000 a year to stash away, I'd suggest setting up a $2000 IRA to be redeemed 42 years hence, at age 72. Next year a separate IRA would be set up for age 73, and so on. The 42 years is a nice conservative hedge against almost any conceivable contingency. If the market returns an inflation adjusted 12%, the $2,000 will make seven turns (doubling every six years) producing a nice pension of $256,000 annually. Of course, if you go for the fast lane with top mutual funds you might achieve 15% net, about 8 turns or roughly $500,000 a year. Then again, the 8% crowd would show you about $60,000 for your efforts. A thirty year old with a working spouse might put away $3,000 a year, providing tax free pensions of $375,000, $750,000 or $90,000 per year, using our three interest assumptions. With age 72 to infinity taken care of, our 30-year-old can discuss with an eager financial planner the need to set up a program to fill the missing years—age 65 to 71. Shouldn't be too tough to do, with 401K maxed to the match, a pathetic Social InSecurity contribution and whatever disposable income can be freed up during the heavy earning years. Our thirty-year-old can look forward to a comfortable retirement without suffering through a Spartan middle age.

The forty-year-old, waking up to the inevitably of old age must really scramble, to the tune of $21,000 a year, to have a good shot at a $100,000 pension, according to *Fortune. Fortune's* readers must all earn well above the median of if they can read this and not retch. For the uneasy *Fortune* reader and the rest of the populace there may be another way.

The Perry approach, as I'm sure you've surmised by now is to designate specific pools of money for very specific future years. Lets have our 40-year-old working couple put $3,000 in a Roth IRA, setting up a new account each year. I prefer Roth because it feels much better to get tax-free money in the September of your life. Mathematically it makes no difference. But you must realize that by putting $3,000 in a Roth IRA you are investing more money than with $3,000 in a regular IRA. The old clunker that your retirement tax rate should be lower is no longer valid. Remember, we're aiming for double your average salary for retirement 'pay.' Moreover, Roths have no mandatory redemption rules starting at age 70.5, as regular IRA's do.

Anyway, the first years $3,000 is designated 2035, thirty-six years hence and our subject's 76th birthday. Thirty-six years is about the minimum you should use to squeeze most of the risk out of the market, and get the real benefit of the time value of money. Similar to our thirty-year-old's calculations above, your money will make 6 turns at 12%, 9 at 18%, and 4 at 8%. This produces a 'pension' of $200,000 at 12%, $1,500,000 at 18%, but only $48,000 at 8%, but all of them tax free. If you are unlucky enough to get only 8% net out of top quality mutual funds over the next 36 years you will be unlucky, indeed. Yet at age 76, your home paid for, your Social InSecurity (if nothing changes) at around $20,000 and with anything else you may have been able to squirrel away, you should be in no danger of having to move in with the kids.

Once these pools have been set up, you should be set for life after 76. To have a reasonable shot at the good life from 65-75 you're going to have to hustle. Obviously you should max out your 401K. You still have 25 years to go, and should resist any urge to sleep well with fixed rate investments. If it makes you nervous get over it. You want a big retirement? Then you can't afford to be a wimp.

Remember we never advocate hot stocks, market tips or arcane investments. If you can't take the time to find a handful of mutual funds with above average long term and recent returns, you don't deserve a gala old age. Individual stocks? Probably not a good idea, but if you're a great picker and an even better seller, build your own fund. I found that I was a very good picker in my youth but a lousy seller. I'd buy, fall in love with my stock, watch it go up, then watch it go down.

When we were 45, my wife Anita and I had near zero net worth. No pension (I was an itinerant data-processing manager) some home equity, but three kids in private colleges simultaneously. We had two goals in 1982. One was to retire at age sixty with a retirement income equal to our final working wages. The second was to see every seeable corner of the world, including visiting all 50 states before our Social InSecurity kicked in. Anita was in charge of funding our world adventures from her teaching salary. If pressure, dedication and contribution to society were the criteria, her salary would have been twice mine. But the world doesn't work that way. Adding to her burden was our agreement that we were too old and creaky to fly coach and our cruises had to be first cabin. After about 40 cruises and innumerable land ventures (never the same place twice) we've just about met our goal. Visiting Hope, Arkansas last year completed our 'nifty 50' state visits and, save for a planned trip along the west coast of Africa, we can say we've been there, done that for just about anywhere anyone would want to go.

Meanwhile, I had to construct a grid showing every year of retirement across the top and every potential source of revenue down the side and fill in the squares. After some false starts (you should see some of my defunct tax shelters), I caught on to the time value of money. Fortunately, my employer was enlightened about retirement and allowed senior people to defer salary to some future point in time and prescribe the nature of pay out. For example, I put a healthy chunk of my 1985 bonus into AmEx stock with its pay out pegged to begin ten years after retirement, with payment spread out over 15 years. If the stock continues to do well, we will get a windfall starting in 2005. Conversely, if AmEx goes bankrupt so do I; non-qualified retirement programs have no legal clout (although some employers insure against this very contingency). It's a risk I'm willing to take. Incidentally, deferred comp plans are not just for top executives. Anita's former school district has a very good plan for teachers. If your employer has no liberal salary deferral program, hassle your Human Resources people or change jobs.

Yes, with a lot of determination and a little luck, and a very retirement savvy and responsive employer, we were able to retire very comfortably at age 62 with retirement income twice our final salary. And literally saw the world in the intervening 13 years. Whatever your goals, you can probably achieve them with a solid approach, an optimistic outlook and a real appreciation for the time value of money.

Retirement Planning for Grandchildren

Let us suppose that you are reasonably comfortable, retired and dote on your very young grandchildren. You would like to do something for them but are well aware that nothing screws up a young person faster than the curse of affluence. Of course you have funds put away to help them significantly when college rolls around, but you do want them to make their own way in life without the burden of your largesse. How about assuring them a very comfortable retirement?

Let's say little Drew, now 3 years old, shows signs of emerging genius (all my grandchildren do, don't yours?) and you want him to follow his heart, even if it doesn't lead to the big bucks. Will those colorful, imaginative childish scrawls eventually evolve into the Van Gogh (with ears) of the 21ˢᵗ Century? Or just another starving artist, brooding in his garret? Perhaps you'll never know if Drew can draw, but it won't matter. To insure his retirement you would, ideally, fund a Roth IRA for each year of his eventual dotage. Small problem; the IRS allows only people with earned income to set up IRA's. They can't be gifted. If you're looking for 'tax cut' ideas to support, a 'kid's IRA', not just for college expenses, should be high on your lobbying list.

Getting around this barrier requires a little ingenuity. The best way would seem to be the new 'educational Roth IRA.' Under Section 529 of the IRS Code, you are allowed to contribute after-tax dollars to a college education IRA. You can put in a huge amount without triggering any gift tax, and it grows tax-free for the beneficiary's college education (no college=big penalty). Your agreement with Drew would be that as soon as he has earned income, he will use it to set up regular Roth IRA's for his retirement. At that time an equivalent amount will be released (or earmarked) from the 'educational IRA' to pay for college expenses. If this is a bit confusing, your accountant can help you out. If you continue this offer until Drew is through college, he can pick up the baton thereafter. Since you have funded ages 65 to 74, he should develop a plan to fund the years 75-150 (yes, he might well live that long). All he has to do is start his own Roth IRA program, ideally by age 25, but hopefully by age 35. His first IRA would be coded Drew Moore—72 (he turns 75 in 2072) and each year thereafter he'll purchase another IRA for each successive year of his eventual golden years. And 'golden' they will be.

We have pegged our growth mutual fund's annual return at 15% gross, 12% net of inflation. A number of funds have done better than that over the past 40 years. We've already agreed that the next 50 years will be 'better'—on balance—than the past 50. Thus 12% annual return appears appropriately conservative. What will Drew's retirement income look like? Disregarding any other savings, 401K, Social InSecurity or whatever, it looks like Drew can retire at age 65 with 'your' retirement IRA's paying him over $1/2 million dollars **totally tax free**, each and every year until he's 75.

When Drew reaches 75 his own retirement program kicks in. Not that it should matter. Presumably Drew, by this time a solid conservative citizen, didn't spend all his $1/2 million a year, non-taxable income over the preceding ten years. Anyway, his conscientious efforts, if he started his $2000 IRA's at age 25 would continue his annual income of about 500 thousand dollars, still tax free, which isn't bad for someone whose house should be paid for by then. If he didn't start until age 35 he'd have to get by on $125,000 a year. If Drew decides to retire early, say at age 56, he'd get about $200,000 dollars a year from your thoughtfulness. His own program, best started at age 25, would produce about a quarter million annual stipend at age 68.

"Aha," you retort, ever the cynic, "inflation will make your $1/2 million worth much less!" Not so, our calculations are in constant dollars, discounting an expected return of 15% by 3% for inflation, even though inflation in our brave new century should average less than 3%. If we didn't use constant dollars, Drew's pay out would be over $2,000,000 (in 2059 dollars) a year. Isn't it interesting that modest 3% inflation will turn two million dollars into half a million dollars of current buying power in about 50 years?

For those of you who harbor the comforting notion that a 'safe' 6% is half as good as an 'expected' 12% we have some bad news. If you followed this timid style of investing, Drew would get instead of a $1/2 million pay out, a paltry $32,000 a year.

Furthermore, where are you going to get a 'safe' 6% net of inflation? There are no 'safe' 9% investments to my knowledge. Government bonds, the safest of all, pay little more than 6% and after deducting 3% for inflation, have a real return of about 3%. That means, effectively, that Drew would draw $8,000 a year instead of $1/2 million. What would you do? Take zero risk for a $8,000 pension, or very modest risk for $1/2 million? Furthermore, if for some reason the world prospered over the next half century but the stock market faltered and returned only 8% in real terms, Drew would still have a handsome pension of near $125,000 a year.

What should you do for Drew? Obviously go for the gold. The upside is so extraordinary. The downside, relatively modest. Yet the mass of mankind appears to have a significant portion of their long-term savings in low return fixed instruments. As we've said, these people should walk around with a lightening rod attached to their backside. For their fears of a draconian stock market collapse are about the same level of risk as lightning striking them out of the blue.

One final note. Suppose you want to help your grandchildren but you are of limited means. You may have only $5000 to spare when Drew is thirteen years old. Shouldn't his college fund have a higher priority? The problem is, the time value of money can't do much in 5 years. You'll probably invest conservatively, as you should. Thus your $5000 might only contribute $6000 or so (constant dollars) toward Drew's education. This won't make, frankly, much impact. But a $5000 investment in his eventual retirement might well make a near million dollar (tax free, constant dollar) difference. You decide which is more important.

IV. Social InSecurity

The Immaculate Misconception

"Save Social Security!" is the mantra of most politicians. They couldn't be more wrong. The insured pension portion of Social Security has become the cruelest hoax ever perpetrated on the American public. To the affluent top quartile of American families, Social Security is almost irrelevant. The second quartile, above the median in family income (about $40,000), gains a bit of luxury from Social Security to brighten an otherwise pedestrian retirement. The third quartile, those of modest means, are most benefited by Social Security, it lifts them out of poverty and into a level of threadbare comfort. The bottom quartile, almost totally dependent on Social Security for retirement income, is effectively kept in a state of economic slavery. Little wonder we changed its name—to 'Social InSecurity.'

TV documentaries and news features on Social Security invariably point out that those currently receiving benefits will receive considerably more than they contributed. The baby boomers will receive a bit more than they paid in over the years and the beleaguered 'Generation X'ers' will receive somewhat less than they 'gave at the office.' This presumably, makes retirees feel good, baby boomers, reconciled and Generation X'ers furious. Truth be known, they should all be furious. And yet the public is very supportive of Social Security. It is a well-managed agency and people are philosophical about poor returns. They think it's good for 'poor' people and are complacent about FICA taxes, which, for many, exceed their income taxes. Of all the misconceptions (savings bonds, savings rates, dividend rates, trade deficit, productivity, etc.), Social Security is indeed the 'immaculate misconception.'

Let's start with a Generation X couple. Both 30 years old, both working and earning about $60,000 a year and contributing about $3,600 each year toward their eventual retirement some 37 years hence. (Remember young people can't start collecting full Social InSecurity until they're 67). At that time, assuming they both kept working, they will receive about $25,000 annually in pension benefits. Is this really good? Is there a better alternative? Let's hypothesize an alternate scenario.

To avoid complicating and confusing the issue, will make all illustrations in constant 1999 dollars. We assume that both benefits and tax contributions will grow over time, roughly in lockstep with inflation. Actually, Social InSecurity will require more then $3,600 (again, in constant dollars) to meet its obligations in the future. For illustrative purposes, however, we will hold the contributions at $3,600 a year giving a slight bias toward Social InSecurity, which enhances the credibility of our arguments. Some experts, nonetheless, claim that diminished benefits or dramatic increases in payroll taxes will be necessary for Social InSecurity to avoid bankruptcy.

Our hypothetical couple will pay $3,600 in payroll taxes each year until they retire, and their employer(s) will match this amount. Again, we will not take into account any increases due to inflation, as this is a constant dollars analysis. We'll present our typical couple with the following scenario: You can stay in the traditional Social InSecurity system, paying your payroll taxes and receiving the traditional benefits. If the current system proves to be under-funded both you payroll taxes and your employer's contribution will increase in real dollars. Your benefits might, but probably won't, decline if SSA faces problems of solvency. You have the alternative, however, of opting out of the Social InSecurity pension system. Each year, upon your instruction, your employer will send your (constant dollar) $3,600 to a reputable financial intermediary of your choosing where it will be invested in an approved equity mutual fund that you have designated. Your employer's contributions will continue to be paid to SSA, without change. You will not be able to access these funds for any reason. In your first year of retirement you will have the initial year's payment returned to you along with whatever dividends, capital gains, or whatever have accrued over the years. Each subsequent year's contribution will similarly be invested in the same or similar manner and paid out in lump sum, fully taxable, on each subsequent year of retirement.

You would make these contributions involuntarily each year of your working life right up to the year you retire, whether it is 60, 67, 75 or whatever. You or your heirs will then receive annual payments for however many years you have contributed.

Your retirement income could vary somewhat from year to year. There is some risk that the vicissitudes of the marketplace could affect you adversely, that a sudden, sharp recession could cost you some of your principal. By comparison, staying with Social InSecurity will pay you $25,000 a year, as long as you live. There are, of course, no Social InSecurity payments to your heirs after you die.

Would you take the risk? If the next 37 years are similar to the last 25 or 30, you will receive a check for about $250,000 to help you survive your first year of retirement. We calculated your investment at 12% compound annually, assuming a 15% gross return and a 3% annual inflation. If we took the actual numbers for the past 25 years the check would be closer to $625,000. But you'd never believe us. Even $250,000 a year, for 37 years is a little hard to swallow, especially considering your alternative action (stick with Social InSecurity) would result in about $25,000 for each year of retirement. Of course the $250,000 is fully taxable; depending on your other income (if any) the Social InSecurity payment would be partially tax free.

But we're not finished. If by some misfortune you pass on after a few lean years on Social InSecurity, your heirs get nothing. Well not exactly. Social InSecurity will send them $255 to bury you. What better, bitter evidence of the anachronism that is Social InSecurity!

In 1935, $255 might have buried you, and most everyone died within a few years of turning 65. The world is different now, and has been for 40 years and no one, it would seem, has noticed. Rather than a paltry $255 final payment, the alternate plan would present your heirs with a check for $250,000 (or so) every year for the remaining years of your retirement plan. In our example, if you paid in for 37 years, retired at 67, died at 72, your heirs would receive $250,000 (in constant dollars) for 32 **additional** years. All of this might well happen if we accept the simple premise that the world will be just a bit better off in 2050 than it is today.

"That's all well and good for the future," you say, "But, in the past Social Security has been a boon for society. I'll bet you can't show a similar scenario for the past." I'll bet I can.

Our belief in Social InSecurity is so fundamental, so pervasive, that even in recent writings, noted economists speculated that Social InSecurity made workers complacent about savings. That Social InSecurity taxes would produce, over time, greater retirement benefits than a worker could have gotten if comparable payments were made into a private pension plan. Therein lies the rub. Private pension plans, in their defined benefit manifestation, are second only to Social InSecurity in their disservice to the 20th century family. We'll discuss defined benefit plans in more detail in another chapter.

I submit that there is not a single entry point in the history of Social InSecurity (since 1935) wherein a new worker wouldn't have retired considerably better off by opting for our alternate plan, had it been available. Did you know that years ago, Federal employees could opt out of Social Security and set up their own retirement program? (Can't anymore, the law was changed in 1983.) Three counties in Texas choose to do so, and studies show these federal retirees are enjoying pensions triple what Social InSecurity would have given them. Our alternative programs calls for investing only about half of current employee payroll taxes in a personal equity pension fund, the rest goes to funding current retirees, disability benefits and the like. Actually, the alternative plan would work pretty well if only 25% of payroll taxes were diverted to the private fund. Whatever the cost, it gets worse each year we procrastinate.

Anyway, back to my contention that Social InSecurity has always been a bad deal for working people. Of course, there weren't any mutual funds in 1935. They are a product of the 50's and didn't really begin to catch on until the 70's. But what would have happened if a typical couple had our option, say, in 1960, (the beginning of the modern world) when mutual funds were available? Jack D. and Rose E. Rivatour earned $25,000 that year and contributed about $300 in payroll taxes. They were a solid, typical middle class family, he a supermarket manager, she originally an assembly line worker, later a junior high teacher. Yes, I know teachers didn't pay Social Security taxes in 1960. Maybe I should make her a junior high janitor, but then I would have to raise the combined income. In the intervening years their salaries did a little better than keeping pace with inflation as did their payroll taxes. When they retired in 1995, their combined salaries had reached about $100,000; their payroll taxes had been near the maximum ($3,000+) for quite some time.

Since neither ever individually paid the maximum tax, I would guess their SS pension to be about $1,000 each per month. Computing their retirement 'kitty' if they had been allowed to invest their portion of the FICA tax (excluding the employer's contribution) in equity mutual funds could be an arduous task. Luckily, their contributions pretty much track the amounts I contributed during my 42 years of salaried toil. My history is spelled out in painful detail in Chapter V. The Rivatours put in a bit more than I did so I think we can safely say they'd accumulate at least a similar $600,000. They could stay fully invested, draw down $50,000 a year and still have it double to $1.2 million in about 10 years. Their pension would be twice as good as Social InSecurity and they build a very nice estate. A rosy retirement indeed.

Even if getting out of Social InSecurity were an option, which it isn't, there is a point, however, after which it is not feasible to opt out. The time value of money means just that—you need time. You would need at least 18 years for your personal pension plan to have a good shot at beating Social InSecurity. In our hypothetical personal pension plan option to Social InSecurity we would have to offer a partial benefit option to older people if we wanted them to opt out of Social InSecurity. The amount of benefit remaining would be scaled for ages 45-55. Beyond that, Social InSecurity is probably the only practical course of action.

You have perhaps noticed that our retirement scenario assumes that elderly people should keep all their retirement funds in growth oriented mutual funds and even put additional money into 'new' growth fund accounts as long as they live. We can't emphasize enough the necessity of keeping fixed income instruments out of long-term retirement programs. Fixed income securities are second only to FICA taxes as the basis for inefficient retirement funding.

The issue is so key that if I were designing the privatized personal retirement program alternate to Social InSecurity, I would not allow 'optees' to select any fixed instruments as a savings vehicle. Nor would I even allow 'balanced funds' be selected until the very final years of a given pool's run. A more practical incentive to guide workers to the proper investment vehicles is to provide 'guarantees' to workers that select appropriate investment vehicles. There might be two classes of investment vehicles. The (A) list would be all the growth mutual funds that achieved a good Morningstar rating and an appropriate return over the past 10 years. The (B) list would include all investments allowed by 401K regulations. If a worker chose the (A) program, the government would guarantee that the eventual pension would at least equal the alternate Social InSecurity benefit. If the pay out fell below Social InSecurity, the Feds would ante up the difference. If a worker selects Plan B, they could invest as they pleased (within reason) with no federal guarantees whatsoever. There are, after all, many different, relatively 'safe' investments that the most timorous can select, sleep well, and receive somewhat more than Social InSecurity promises.

If an optional private pension system were offered today's pre-retirees, how would the current Social InSecurity be funded? We'd have to find up to $3,600 in new government revenue for each person opting for a private pension. This is apart from possible increases in the payroll taxes percentages that many experts insist will be necessary. In that case, we'll all pay higher payroll taxes, whether in or out of the system.

If half the taxpayers opt out of Social Security (approx. 50 million) we'll have to find another $50-150 billion each year for more years than I care to count, maybe 30 or so. But the present system is far worse and gets 'worser' every year. Today's budget surpluses are projected to grow. They could absorb much of the shortfall. A few additional budget cuts and we're there.

In a perfect world, we could provide an alternate privatized system. But it's not going to happen. The economics of a complete switchover are just too daunting. Major reforms can be contemplated, although they may have to be gradual to be accepted. Read on.

Social InSecurity Reform

The Black-American Political Action Committee (BAPAC) has been running commercials espousing privatized Social InSecurity, as well they might. Their constituency certainly has a fair representation of those victimized by Social InSecurity (Republican presidential hopefuls Stephen Forbes and John McCain advocate a similar position).

To begin with, the SS payroll tax is regressive. A semi-skilled tile bonder making $16,000 a year, not much more than minimum wage, contributes 6% or $1,000 annually to Social InSecurity. A semi-skilled bond trader making $600,000 a year contributes $4,500, less than 1% annually to Social InSecurity. The bond trader feels nothing, neither paying the $4,500 a year, nor in collecting $16,000 a year many years hence.

Joe Lunchbucket, the wage worker feels much pain. The thousand bucks a year could make a big difference. What it does do is make him eligible for a $6,000 a year pension. Can he retire to Florida on $6,000 a year, plus whatever he can earn part-time? No way. He's locked into a dreary life followed by a dismal retirement. And he might live to be 100. At the very least it will feel like 100.

But what if Joe had been allowed to divert his annual $1,000 contribution to a tax deferred fund invested in equities? Much like a 401K, except the money cannot be touched before age 60. What would happen?

Let's assume that his wages grow with inflation over the years. He starts working at age 17 and doesn't stop, except for a few bouts of unemployment, until he's 65. Lets give him 45 working years, having deducted 3 years for all the short periods of unemployment. To make the calculations simple and meaningful, we'll consider his initial $16,000 salary to be his lifetime salary, for indeed it is, in constant dollars. He'll keep up with inflation but will unlikely beat it. This doesn't totally jibe with our contention that our world will get better. But, keeping his salary low merely enhances our argument.

If his $1,000 were invested in a solid growth mutual fund, it would grow at least 15% a year (net of inflation) if we use the market performance of the last 25 years. But we'll use 12%, the S & P index growth history, to keep the analysis conservative.

Starting in his 65th year, Joe Lunchbucket would receive a check for $14,000 (less income tax withholding) each **month** for the following **48** years. That's when he's 113 years old. Actually, if he is thoughtful enough to keep putting away the $1,000 a year (in a Roth IRA, if he has at least $1000 in part time earnings) after the Social InSecurity system stops collecting from his wages, he'll get $14,000 (tax free) a month, 'forever.' Now, we know he won't live forever. When he dies, however, the new system sends his heirs $14,000 a month. For how long? For another 48 years, of course! And if he dies prematurely, his family has a tax-free cushion to keep them going as well as traditional Social Security widow's benefits.

This all sounds like madness. A wage slave earning $16,000 a year, never able to save a dime, never able to scrape together enough for even a minimum down payment on a minimum home (even if someone would give him a mortgage). And then he retires, with a 'pension' that would pay him every month nearly as much as he earned each year of his working life. [Actually, he would probably jump at the age 60 retirement option. Even though it would mean only a paltry $10,000 a month.]

Even though the 21st Century should be as good or better than the last half century, most of us can't accept the notion that an investment in equities could produce such returns. Let's try it at a more 'rational' number. At 8% net annual growth, Joe would retire at about $5,000 a month (ten times his expected Social InSecurity pay out). Let's get truly absurd. If equities return only 4% over the next half-century, Joe will still get $3,000 a month—for 48 years, and again his heirs might also get a similar windfall. Compare this to Social InSecurity's $500 a month while living, then a lump sum ($255) for a gala funeral.

Do you really think that stocks might return only 4%, or even 8% over the next half century with a world hungry for capital, with trade barriers crumbling, war 'banned,' recessions mild and rare, depression non-existent, crime inconsequential and longevity spiraling? Doesn't seem very consistent, does it?

You're probably beginning to suspect that Social InSecurity has outlived its usefulness. Reform is not a case of trust fund solvency. Even a healthy Social Security Administration gives the unskilled wage earner a cruel reward. And many 'reforms' being suggested will **reduce** benefits and push back the retirement date.

Some analysts predict that the Social InSecurity tax will increase to 15.8% by 2050 if benefits and eligibility remain the same as they are today. That is 31.6% counting your employee's contribution. Those analysts have probably overlooked the fact that sometime in the next 50 years the life expectancy of our citizens will probably increase dramatically, far beyond current actuarial expectation. What would this mean? A 60% total tax rate?

When 'reforms' are discussed they, invariably, deal only with delaying the inevitable bankruptcy and skyrocketing tax rate. The President's idea about investing some of the SSA's trust fun in equities was simply a delaying tactic. And, not a very palatable idea, at that. No one wants the government playing the market.

Those of us who have earned well above the median can fashion our own retirement. We, also, are more likely to benefit from 401K programs, company pensions, and might well pay off our home mortgage before we retire. Social InSecurity is a nice bonus, but hardly essential.

The low-income worker gets no pension, no 401K and usually has no home. Social InSecurity delivers so little to one that needs so much. Yet, all the discussion seems aimed at delivering even less. At the same time, the comparable low-income worker in Great Britain and Chile is contributing similar amounts to a government sponsored privatized pension plan. Although only 19 years old, the Chilean social pension program, despite its flaws, is earning a consistent 13% in each of its three conservatively managed portfolios. Jose Lunchbucket, who earns $10,000 a year, and will never save a peso on his own, can look forward to retiring on a pension worth up to **25 times** his annual wage. His American counterpart, earning near twice as much, but contributing an equivalent amount to Social Security, is guaranteed a pension worth almost **half** his modest pay. Yet we seem so content. It's enough to break your heart. Doesn't anyone care?

Throughout this treatise, we have suggested that only the minimum wage, unskilled workers are incapable of properly funding a reasonable retirement and are at the mercy of government programs. The sad truth is that many, many people, some earning well above the median are totally incapable of accumulating any significant funds for retirement. Some have 'too many' children, some have chronic health problems, some have elderly parents to support and many are congenitally incapable of saving a dime. Theirs will not be happy golden years. If you're a senior (or even an elderly junior), you, I'm sure, will avow that you want a better world for your children and grandchildren. Here's your chance to take a positive stand. Put your tax reduction where your mouth is. Think about all the young people under 18 today. They will start to retire around 2050 and will all be retired around 2070. Would you like to (almost) guarantee that they will all retire with a base annual retirement of at least $125,000 and for many (in constant dollars) $250,000 or more? This is without regard to their earning ability, their career path, whether they make minimum wage or 'Wall Street' money. You can make this happen by hounding your Congress people to support the following:

When a person signs up for a Social Security number he/she becomes eligible for the new private SS pension plan, wherein, the first $1000 in payroll taxes each year is directed to the individuals private pension plan. The money must be invested in an approved equity mutual fund and cannot be touched for any reason, until at least 36 years have passed, and the person is at least 60 years old. Moreover, any year the new young enrollee doesn't have $1000 in payroll tax (i.e. gross earnings are less than $16,000) the individual, or others acting in his/her behalf can make up the difference with a tax-deductible contribution.

A 'generation X'er' starting at age 24 would complete the 36-year requirement by age 60 and could immediately receive a pension of about $65,000 if the better mutual funds achieve only a 12% (net) annual growth. If a youngster starts at 16 and lets it ride until age 64, the pension would be a mighty $250,000 a year. All of this has nothing to do with how his/her life is spent or misspent. As long as annual earnings reach $16,000 (to produce a $1000 tax) or someone ante's up the deficiency. The time value of money will serve them well. What does this cost you, our noble senior? Not much. No tax reduction this year. No budget surplus perhaps. No huge army. No big deal!

Wait a minute. What about all the people already working? Especially those only in the workforce a year or two. No problem. Everyone is eligible. But they must follow the rules. They must relinquish all claim to normal SS retirement benefits and each year the first $1000 of payroll tax must be invested for 36 years, regardless of the individual's current age.

What are the economic consequences of such a plan? If there are 50 million 'youngish' workers that opt for this program, SSA's revenues will drop by $50 billion a year. In return, the SSA has no pension obligation to these people whatsoever.

If we hypothesize that 'everyone' under 40 joins up, and 'no one' over 40 signs up, we find that by 2050 SSA is paying out relatively little (only to those people over 90) and by 2060 to an even smaller group. But won't they be still collecting 12% of the nation's total payroll every year? One would hope not, of course, but what we do have is an opportunity to amortize, to smooth out, the total cost over the next 70 years.

It is relatively easy for actuaries to calculate the total cost for the next seventy years and what the average cost per year would be. Even if they do grossly underestimate longevity in the 21st century. Real costs during the first 35 years will be huge, far beyond the 'average' but when the costs begin to drop over the last 35 years, the deficit can be paid off.

This suggests that the initial $50 billion a year shortfall might be amortized over the entire 70 years, at which point, SSA would go out of the insured pension business. Even if we must ante up the 50 billion each year, it is not too tough. Forget the tax cut (except perhaps the estate tax portion).It is primarily for people that are already comfortable, and speaking for that group, I say we do not need it!

Using budget surpluses to pay down the national debt is an exercise in futility. It will cut itself in half every 24-36 years, anyway (inflation). And, of course, maintaining a monstrous military is something any intelligent public should refuse to do. Thus we have several options for raising the money that might be necessary to get SSA over the 'hump,' during the transition. There is no reason why a new privatized Social Security should in any way compromise present pensioners or anyone else that stays with the old system. We know that the Social Insecurity System is an insurance system, not welfare, and is not supported in any way by general Federal revenues. This warm fuzzy has outlived its usefulness. SSA collects a harsh, regressive tax and fixing it, once and for all by using general tax revenue dollars is no longer onerous.

V. The Privatized Pension System

Reform Alternatives

Finding $50 billion or more a year to fund a reformed Social InSecurity shortfall is a substantial problem. As a practical political issue it alone could kill any attempt at privatization. But there is hope. Let's take a look at the entire spectrum of workers, not just new entrants, and take a slightly different approach.

We have established that a real return of 12% on equities could be achieved if 2000-2050 is going to be as good or better than 1950-2000. Actually we could argue that 15% is closer to reality.

If so, we have an opportunity to 'reform' Social InSecurity in a manner that will substantially reduce the cost of switching from an abominable system to one that offers all citizens a rational, comfortable retirement. The system might work something like this:

Each worker will be offered the opportunity of opting out of Social InSecurity retirement and having a portion of his/her annual FICA tax directed to a private investment program. The program would invest the 'contribution' in an approved equity mutual fund and would not be subject to any withdrawals, for any reason, before the appropriate retirement date.

As you know every worker's income is subject to a 6.2% payroll tax, for the first $76,000 or so of salary. This does not include the Medicare tax, which is technically another Social Security tax on top of the 6.2% paid into the retirement fund. Your employer kicks in an amount equal to what you 'contribute,' again, 6.2% of the first $76,000 of salary.

In the following, we are suggesting that a portion of 'your' 6% be directed toward a private retirement fund. You would then opt out of Social InSecurity retirement benefits. Social InSecurity also funds disability income for people that can't work and funds for young widows and their children. You would not lose your rights to these payments if you ever qualify.

From ages 16-29, 2% of the worker's total wages would be directed to the investment program. At age 30, the ante might be raised to 3%, and then to 4% after age 40.Certainly, one entering the new system after age 30 deserves a break for contributing during the wonder years ad getting virtually nothing in return. Similarly, someone giving up their Social InSecurity benefits and entering the privatized system after age 40 should be able to deduct at least 4% during the remaining working years.

Even if the under 30 entrant never gets beyond 2% (a low fat pension, indeed) and averages only $15,000 throughout his lifetime, his pension should still be considerably better than the Social InSecurity alternative. Using our 12% equity return assumption for the next half century, his pension would be a robust $40,000 a year ($300 a year, 7 turns over 42 years). This is better than a guaranteed $6,000 Social InSecurity dole, don't you think? Should he take the risk?

We'll go one better. At retirement age 70, our minimum wage earner would be given an option and a guarantee. He could opt for a lifetime fixed annuity (offered by a bevy of eager insurance companies) of about $25,000. Furthermore, he would be guaranteed that if the fixed annuity paid out less than he would have received had he stayed in the old Social InSecurity system, our munificent federal government would, every year, make up the difference. A single person with no heirs might well take this offer. All others might be better served by taking a properly planned annual distribution, with the balance growing smartly (probably more than the distribution) giving our lowly worker a halcyon retirement for 50 years or more at three times the annual income that he made in his most productive working years. You may have noticed that my formula has our intrepid retiree working 45 years. Actually, a low paid worker would presumably start work at age 17 or 18 and work for over 50 years. But would you have believed me if I told you that a person averaging $15,000 a year over a working lifetime might retire with a pension of over $80,000 a year, forever?

What about the guarantee? Could it happen? Not likely, but it could happen. If equities earn less than 4% over the next 50 years, the Feds may have to kick in a little. The risk premium to fund the guarantee would be a pittance. Thus our lowest paid worker would contribute an amount equal to 10% of his pay (4% himself, 6% in matching funds from his employer) to help those who were currently receiving SS retirement benefits and have no alternative. Think about this for a while and it may dawn upon you what an abominable Ponzi scheme our Social InSecurity system has become.

As we have noted, if the best managed equity mutual funds can't return 4% over the next 50 years, our premise is in trouble (that's not all that's in trouble, brother).Yet zillions of people 'invest' their life savings in Government Bonds that pay 4% interest (net of inflation) or less. These people probably rationalize that a sleep-well 6% guaranteed is worth it to them, compared to twice the potential of an equity fund. But 6% compounded over a working lifetime isn't half the interest earned at 12%. It isn't even 1/10 as good. If you don't understand this go back and review the 'time value of money' chapter over and over until you get it.

Moreover those that think 6% is totally safe verses a 'speculative' 12% (in their minds) are stuck in a depression mentality. The probability that the best funds produce significantly less than 6% over the next 50 years is in the same neighborhood of the probability that the federal government goes bankrupt and defaults on those beautiful 6% treasuries.

People that enter the system later in life, still earning minimum level wages, don't do as well. If thirty-year-olds are allowed a 3% allocation to private funds they will 'pension out' at about $30,000 a year; at 4% it would be close to $40,000.

Forty year olds need at least 4% (i.e. 2/3 of the payroll taxes) to see any advantage (a $10,000 pension vs. the government's $5,000) and for fifty year olds it's almost hopeless. Twenty years isn't enough time in the 'time value of money' to get the most value. To be equitable, the policy wonks at SSA should figure out some formula that would allow older people the option of freezing their retirement benefit at current levels with the opportunity to invest a portion of their future contributions to achieve a significantly higher pay out. A delayed retirement date could also work for some. Most older low wage earners would likely be too 'chicken' to opt for a partially privatized pension and this is probably OK.

Incidentally, in all our calculations we have expressed pension dollars in constant dollars. Certainly in 50 years inflation (even if only a minuscule 1.5-2% a year) will cut the real value of anyone's Social InSecurity in half. This is why Social InSecurity payments go up a little each year, as does the cap on wages subject to Social InSecurity taxes. We have assumed that the low wage earner will never improve his standard of living, in real terms his wages will remain constant. We hope this isn't true and our premise that the world will improve over the next half century suggests that it won't be true. Thus when we say a worker 50 years from now will receive a pension of $30,000 in 1999 dollars, we are being properly conservative. He would likely receive considerably more than $60,000 in 2050 dollars.

Planning Retirement
without Privatized Social Security

The more affluent worker will have several options while awaiting a change in federal retirement legislation. We will assume that most families earning above the current median income ($40,000) are well versed in the wisdom of maximizing 401K and IRA opportunities.

The 401K is particularly important for the comfortable family's retirement plan. One dumb thing a person can do is fail to opt for 401K salary deductions at least to the level of the employer match A dumber thing a person can do is invest his 401K money in a fixed income vehicle [money fund, GIC (guaranteed investment contract), federal income fund or the like]. It's somewhat irrational for a 35-year-old to invest retirement funds in fixed instruments, which will compound at less than 6% over the ensuing 35 years. Tragically, that's just what many do. Go back and reread our treatise on how 12% equity funds could produce 10 times as much in 35-40 years then will ever-so-safe government bonds.

401k's are notoriously biased against the young and the restless low paid worker. Companies must find ways to make 'unattractive' employees ineligible. If groups that have a poor participation history are not screened out, they bring the averages down and consequently, in keeping with 401k regs, the executive group cannot contribute the maximum percentage to their own retirement accounts. Thus part-timers, those under 21, and short timers are often disqualified. The net result is that most young people reach age 30 (having averaged 8-10 jobs each) with next to nothing in their retirement accounts. But when I see statistics on how many reasonably paid people don't opt for 401K deductions at the matching maximum, and the percentage of all 401K contributions that go into fixed income instruments, I am inclined to rethink my belief that our native intelligence has grown appreciably over the last century or two. Perhaps the world improves without a proportionate growth in intellect. I did notice that every day 8,000 teens take up smoking, thus replenishing the ranks of the stupid. Maybe intelligence has yet to achieve critical mass.

In the realm of dopey investing, taking too much risk in 401K planning can be even more ruinous. In 1978 my employer, the venerable Home Insurance Company inaugurated a munificent 401K that had a generous 3 to 1 match. That is, for every $18 the employee put away the company would match it with a $6 contribution. The catch was that the only investment vehicle provided was company stock, which coincidentally, was selling at that time for about $24. Employees rejoiced, imagine buying stock at 25% discount with no broker's commission!

Many did so, up to the maximum salary deduction allowed. I recently looked up Home Insurance stock. It was about 75 cents. The company was no longer venerable. It was hardly viable. Many who had conscientiously done the right thing saw their retirement dreams collapse. This is the kind of risk that one should not take. It is rational to believe that the market will not collapse over the next fifty years and will shrug off occasional 'corrections.' It is not rational to believe that any given company will still be prosperous 50 years, even 20 years hence. I can think of several Dow 30 companies whose stock I would be loath to put my hard earned employee salary in because they might well be on the down slope of their 'S' curve within that time frame.

Having said all this I will admit to putting every dime I could scrounge up into my employer's stock in 401K and other deferred comp vehicles. But when American Express stock tanked in the 1987 'correction' I mightily blanched. It lost half its value in a few weeks. We struggled back to par a few years later only to find the "Barbarians at the Gate" had roundly smacked the idiots within. Another 50% loss. Again, teeth gritting time. All's well that ends well, of course, but you better have a cast iron stomach if you take this kind of risk. Certainly Home Insurance, a mediocre company in its best days was never any American Express. I also knew that our piece of American Express

(IDS) was growing its earning at 20% a year without wavering. In 1983 a $50 million dollar profit operation would (since I understood the time value of money) produce a billion dollars bottom line in the year of the millenium.

This could offset a lot of arrogant hubris in the 'house of (credit) cards.' They did in fact, learn humility and restored their winning ways, (with IDS alumnus, Harvey Golub at the helm) and IDS, now called American Express Financial Advisors, is right on track.

The more efficient wage earners that maximize their 401K in a recognizable growth mutual fund and put something away in IRA's is well ahead of the game. If they view Social InSecurity as a supplement to their basic retirement plan there is much they can do to maximize their income during their golden years. And 'golden years' is being redefined. Back in '35 when social security was inaugurated most people didn't live to 65 and those that did, few collected a pension for very many years thereafter. Back in the sixties, I reviewed the pension experience of my employer and found that the retirees lived on average to age 67. And they had the nerve to promulgate a dreadfully inadequate defined benefit retirement program.

The old fashion pension program is fast becoming a relic, a manifestation of the good old days when conventional wisdom suggested that retiring at 50% of our final salary was about all we should hope for. Defined benefit programs reflected that thinking by awarding 1.5% of final average salary for each year of employment. If you stayed with one employer for forty years (you daredevil you!) your pension might be as much as 60% of final salary.

Defined contribution pension systems (401K's for most, 403B for the not-for-profit sector) achieved popularity in the 80's when companies decided to limit their liability by matching employee deposits to a pre-set limit and leaving investment choice to the whim of the employee. Somewhat ironically this happened at a time when market performance had significantly outpaced actuarial expectation. It never occurred to many companies to increase pension benefits to offset rampant inflation. One of the cruelest aspects of defined benefit was to have inflation ravage someone's pension, which, unlike Social InSecurity, probably had no cost of living escalator.

Defined benefit was becoming irrelevant to a mobile workforce. A migrant data processing manager myself, keeping just a step ahead of vengeful superiors for most of my working life, I arrived at my final employer at age 48 without a nickel of vested pension benefits. In any event, defined contribution plans are portable and itinerant workers can roll them over to a new employer's 401K. Some employers paternalistically provide defined benefit as well. The 'reformed' defined benefit plans allow a cash buyout option at retirement. In my case, my final employer offered me $250,000 to be rolled over into an IRA or $20,000 for life. I thought I could do better than 8% a year and have the capital intact when I died, so I rolled over. You presumably would do a similar analysis and decide which option suits your risk profile and situation. Companies switching to cashout plans often do so at the expense of older workers during the transition period.

Cash balance pensions, supposedly biased toward the young worker aren't much kinder to kids than are the 401K's. Most young people are notoriously peripatetic, and are often eliminated by 5 year vesting rules. When they finally settle in, at least for 5 years per employer, (and cash balance is portable thereafter) they tend to be well into their 30's. This does great mischief to the 'time value of money' which may only have 30 years or so to do its magic. The cash balance pension looks good on paper but may not deliver. Let's suppose your company puts away 3% of your salary every year, a reasonably generous plan, and credits the account with 6.5% interest (a typical amount) every year. You begin working for this benevolent employer at age 28, the pension plan kicks in a year later and, unlike many workers, you plan to stay forever. Your salary is $50,000 and will only rise with inflation, with typical raises of 2-3% a year. We'll keep your salary at $50,000 to make a constant dollar analysis.

Many pension funds have brilliant managers, but even if Peter Lynch runs your fund, you'll probably get 6.5% interest regardless of the funds performance. Your employer is not about to take any performance risk. Who gets the excess if the fund performs far beyond 6.5%? Don't ask. Anyway, after putting in $1500 a year your pension at age 65 would be about $12,000. Whoopee! Of course, you could roll it over into an IRA.

When 401K's first appeared, there was considerable hand wringing in the financial press over the possibility that the naive employee would mismanage his retirement with risky investment choices. The problem is quite the opposite. Better than 50% of all 401K funds are in fixed instruments, which are the least desirable means of building long term portfolios. And, except for aberrations like the Home Insurance stock debacle, companies tend to offer rather reasonable equity investments to their minions.

Far more deleterious are some practices of some defined benefit programs. As I was preparing to leave my first employer after a disagreement (they wanted to show me the door; I already knew where it was) I lamented to a fellow sufferer that the 20 year vesting rule left me with no pension rights after 17 years of service. "Don't feel bad," he replied, "even if you were vested you'd get nothing." "How so?" "Well, you get 1.5% per year of service, which on a 1970 salary of $25,000 is about $6000. But don't forget this program has a 50% Social Security offset. So if your SS benefit in 1997 were to be $12,000, you'd receive only the pension amount above $6000. Six thousand minus six thousand leaves you with a zero pension."

'Gotchas' like this and the even more insidious lack of cost of living escalators make such pension plans a poor vehicle for golden year's glory. One of the tenets of this book is that the 'retire at half pay' bromide is totally inadequate and unnecessary. Our goal is retire at twice your final salary, but you won't get there with Social Insecurity and ill-defined benefit pension plans.

Today's 50 year old, healthy and with no genetic monsters under their bed is odds-on, in my opinion, to live to 100. I can't prove it quite yet but the reasons why I think so are in the 'futures chapter.' To-day's 40 year old, with similar caveats, may well see 120 before they can't be differentiated from the vegetation. How does one plan a retirement of up to 60 years after the gold watch presentation?

The easy way is to sit down with a qualified financial planner. Tell the planner all about your financial wherewithal, plans, and goals. Don't discuss 12% long-term returns with them. It makes them nervous and makes their compliance people physically ill. Do ask them what the last 10 years, or inception to date, returns are for their favorite mutual funds.

Your planner will help you quantify your goals and your expected income up until your demise, which they like to peg at 80 or 85. If you don't have the wherewithal to produce the desired income until your judgement day, you'll work together on means of increasing your savings.

It's then up to you to figure out what you'll do if you live beyond your target age. To divert for a moment, I once invented a product to meet this need. I called it 'insurance against living too long.' In planning your retirement, you're faced with a dilemma. If you're terrified that you'll live too long and end up penniless you will plan to live off the interest on your capital and not touch the principal. The problem with this strategy is that you might live like a church mouse for a few years, drop dead, and your worthless nephew gets a huge windfall, which he promptly dissipates. The alternative is living high off the hog until the money runs out and you aren't as dead as you expected to be. Then you're stuck trying to live off whatever modest Social InSecurity or other pension benefits you have that go on in perpetuity. Our product, actually called Retirement Assurance was an annuity that kicked in at a predetermined age. For example, you're age 50 now and want to have

$50,000 a year for a comfortably retirement, beginning at age 65. Your planner runs the numbers and reports that you can do so, but your money will run out at age 86, after which you'll have to get by on your anticipated $10,000 a year Social Security benefit. To avoid this unpleasant contingency you would buy a Retirement Assurance annuity that would pay you $40,000 a year, for the rest of your life starting on your 86th birthday. The cost of this product would be but a fraction of the cost of a regular annuity because most of the people that buy the product wouldn't be alive at their target date and everyone's contribution would be spread amongst the survivors. Sort of a 'last man' club or 'Tontine' as they were called before last man insurance pools were banned decades ago.

Pundits loved it; *Forbes* magazine gave it a half page. The public? Forgedaboutit! "You mean to tell me if I buy this and then die I get nothing?" was a common response. "Look stupid" (I thought but never said), "You paid for homeowner's insurance this year. If your house doesn't burn down will you demand you premium back?" That's different, of course.

Our sales people said "Who else has this product so we can compare ours against theirs?" "Nobody has this. It's innovative. You've been telling us the company isn't innovative enough." "But we only want innovations that other companies have and our clients ask for. This requires too much explanation."

Needless to say the product had a short life and a quiet death. I tried to revive interest in a variation tied to Nursing Home insurance. As you know, Nursing Home insurance is pretty expensive but will give you a fairly comfortable last 5 years if you eventually need help and are afraid you'll end up in a Medicaid snake pit if you don't take precautions. If you never go into a nursing home you won't collect a penny, much like my ill-fated Retirement Assurance. But what if you could buy a rider that changed the nursing home pay out to begin when you enter the home, or reach a predetermined very old age, say 95?

In this case if you stayed healthy until a ripe old age, you would collect a considerable annual stipend to cushion your very golden years and perhaps hire the help you need to stay in your own home during those twilight years. The additional premium shouldn't be prohibitive.

In any event, you can't buy insurance against living too long, so you'll need some other way of funding the years after your planner's target date for your demise. You can buy nursing home insurance but the premium will be about $1,000 per person, per year if you're 50 and $2,000 if your 60. And this only buys you the last 5 years in a nice nursing home, if you need to be there.

An attractive alternative if you have time, is to establish 'late life' funds on your own. You need a minimum of 30 years, so if you're 60 and your planner says the money will be gone at 85, you have a small problem. If you're 50 and are a 'party of two' you could set up Roth IRA's each year for specific years 36 years hence. Investing $2,000 this year (the equivalent of annual nursing home insurance premiums) might get you $128,000 (yes, constant dollars) in 2035, the year of your 85th birthday—if, of course, you put the money in a reliable S & P Index Fund. Go for a leading growth fund and you might have $250,000. How do you spend $250,000 when you're 85? And it is all tax-free. The mind fairly boggles.

Each year, of course, you will fund another kitty for the next successive elder year. The beauty in this approach is in its total flexibility and the money is always yours (or your heirs). If you started with $4,000 a year at age 60 and your planner proves prescient and you run out of money at 84, not to fear. You can tap your funds one 'turn' early—receiving $64,000 in 2029. Not too shabby for a couple of codgers with their home paid for, and dragging $15,000 from Social InSecurity, to boot.

If you plan to set up new 'Roths' after you retire, it is imperative that you have equivalent earned income each year after being put out to pasture. Just working enough to receive a W-2 for 2-3 thousand dollars will do it. Even better would be to use your influence in Washington to liberalize the earned income IRA rule as we have discussed in regard to "kid's IRA's."

It might be prudent to keep setting up these funds for years long after you expect to "shuffle off this mortal coil." To begin with, your coil may be less mortal than you thought. If you do exit on your 'use before' date, you have established some pretty fine portfolios for your heirs. If your estate isn't large they can use these funds without paying estate taxes. Besides estate taxes should disappear for most people in the next few years. Seniors become a near majority in the foreseeable future and are very much in favor of much higher estate tax exclusions. Our politicians are certainly loath to ignore this pressure and make the elders hostile!

How a Privatized Social Security Might Have Worked for Me

I started my full time working career in late 1954, as a programmer for the Travelers Insurance Company in Hartford for the munificent sum of $60 a week. At that time, there weren't many real computers around, so I 'programmed' punched card calculators until stored program machines arrived a year or so later.

Recently, I asked the Social Security Administration for a historical printout of all my wages subject to payroll taxes and the amount withheld. I'm sure you've done this yourself, and if you haven't, you should. They have a special request postcard for just this purpose. If you've been around for awhile, it's an interesting document, and even if you haven't, it's comforting to see that they're doing it right. Prior to 1954, I made sporadic contributions to Social Security from summer jobs and other part time work. These funds were not used in any calculation, but I did use them in my analysis to raise the '55 through '59 deposits up to an even $100 a year.

I then set about to figure out what would have happened to me if a privatized Social Security system was in effect back in 1954, assuming that all subsequent contributions would have gone into an equity mutual fund for my eventual retirement, instead of into the government's general coffers. I assumed my employee's matching annual payroll tax would continue to be collected for other SS purposes such as disability and widow's payments, and would not be affected by my calculations.

My next problem was selecting an appropriated investment vehicle. The mutual fund records I have only go back to 1969. There were some mutual funds in 1954, but not many. I decided that from 1954—1969 my deposits would earn at the historical rate of the S & P 500 index for those years. This information I do have. For 1969 and beyond my hypothetical investments were made into the IDS New Dimensions Mutual Fund, which has been a very good (but not the best) performer over the past 30 years.

As you know, this book does not allow any mathematical calculations that cannot be done in my head or on my fingers. For this exercise, however, I had to bend a little and allow a scratch pad.

Now, if there really was a privatized Social Security in 1954, I would have selected a mutual fund and the deposits would be dumped in, year after year, creating an enormous pot of money from which I would draw my 'pension' when I turned 65. Calculating what this pot would be and how much to draw out for each year of retirement is an immense mathematical task, which I may tackle later on in this chapter.

The technique I use (perhaps you've noticed) is to set up each year of deposit as a separate account to be liquidated in its turn 42 years later. In 1955 I was 23 and would retire 42 years later. Thus the 1955 money grew into an amount cashed in during 1997; the 1956 deposit would be redeemed in 1998 and so on. The total of all these little accounts, set up one a year, for 42 years, is exactly the same as dumping all the deposits in one big pot, using, of course, the same growth rates for any given intervening year, regardless of how many pots of money are involved.

The only distortion my technique produces is that the eventual pay outs could widely differ from year to year. Since I put in only $100 in 1955, it's going to produce far less in 1997 than the $2000 I put in, in 1984, produces in 2026.

The chart on page 102 shows what might have happened to the money. It is interesting to note that back in 1955 my contribution was the maximum deduction when my salary was $60 a week, and every year thereafter I paid in the maximum deduction. Thus, my social InSecurity checks this year add up to approximately $16,000, about the most anyone can collect. My social InSecurity will always be about $16,000 in constant dollars, although the actual amount will grow, roughly in pace with inflation.

To keep the calculations from driving me mad, I decided to use 12%, the historical S & P 500 return, until I switched to the 'New D' fund in 1968. All of the calculations prior to today need not be adjusted for inflation since they are real numbers, and are money in the bank. It's only when we project forward do we have to account for the impact of future inflation.

As you can see, New D produced some very fine returns, particularly for the last 25 years, when it hovered around 18 –20%. Going forward, however, I felt in the interest of conservatism, I should not use New D's historical record. I decided instead to use the S & P *inflation adjusted* return for the last 20 years, which happens to be about 12%.

There are some very interesting conclusions one can draw from the chart. The most obvious is that Social InSecurity is really dreadful. Look at the first five years of retirement. My system pays out about the same as the Social InSecurity system. But in those days S.S.A. was only taking 100 bucks a year from me, and giving me back $16,000 forty-two years later. That's about as good as I could do investing the money on my own.

What does this tell you? It says that if Social Insecurity took $100 from you every year and never changed the deduction amount, a pension of $16,000 a year would be a most fine return. But that didn't happen. The deduction grew by bounds and leaps in the seventy's and they ran amok in the eighty's and ninety's. If $100 a year is the right number, they are taking out 36 times the correct amount. That's how bad Social InSecurity is. It pays you back 1/36 (less than 3%) of what it should. Now do you see how naive it is when people say they would be satisfied if they take out of Social InSecurity what they put in?

Note that when SSA deductions were low and growing slowly, the eventual 'pension' my system would produce would be a healthy but not immodest monthly sum. But when deductions skyrocketed, I could look forward to being the most flush old codger in town. Even as a 'young codger,' I'd be in the 'suburbs' of Fat City.

"That's all well and good," I can hear you thinking, "but how much would you actually have in your retirement kitty if SSA had allowed you to put all of your FICA tax into these investments?" Well it's a lot of work, especially without a calculator, but I figured it out and it's about $600,000.

How does $600K compare with my current SSA lifetime annuity of approximately $16,000 a year? Well, I probably could buy a lifetime annuity that would pay me $50,000 a year until I die. That makes it 3+ times as good as Social InSecurity. But I wouldn't do that. I'd stay fully invested. I might take $60,000 out each year and let the rest grow. If I could invest it for a 15% return, my kitty would grow 5% a year and be worth over a million dollars in less than 15 years. How much better than Social InSecurity is this?

You'll note that I've shown how to keep the ball bouncing after retirement (actually, I retired at 63) and payroll taxes are no longer collected. I simply set up a Roth IRA ($2000, I still have some earned income) each year, planning to cash in each one 42 years after its inception. Here's a bonus; it is all tax-free! When I'm 105 I'll really start living grand.

More realistically, my heirs will get a windfall, much of it tax free, each and every year for 42 years—if we choose to set up trusts that way. We haven't said much about the value of the death benefit under privatization (SS has a one-time death benefit of $255). But if I die at my normal 'expiration date' (about 2012), my heirs will receive the payments from 2013-2037 (see chart—forget the 'Roth years' for this analysis). These payments, using only 12% compounding for future years, adds up to more than **$14 million.** Quite a difference.

Seniors are often characterized as being very concerned about the world they'll leave behind and the welfare of their scions. Yet, AARP sometimes lobbies for initiatives that can only cater to senior greed. Taking the estate tax exemption up to $10 million or so is a worthy goal but if AARP were really concerned about future generations, they would campaign mightily for Social InSecurity privatization. They would support the use of budget surpluses to offset the inevitable shortfall during the transition to a private pension system. At the very least they should holler for "Kid's Retirement IRA's." Although neither effort has any beneficial effect on today's seniors, it doesn't harm them either. It would be the noblest legacy that AARP could bestow on its future members.

Have I been unfair to my much-maligned Social InSecurity? Let's try one final test. Suppose I was born 50 years earlier and started work in 1900 at age 18. Imagine that I survived wars and plagues and worked throughout the depression. Accept, also, the premise that Social Security existed in 1900 and an optional private pension was available in much the manner as I have described.

Where would I be when I retired in 1948? After 5 decades of world wars, plague and the millenium's most dreadful depression, my privatized plan would reward me with a pension better than twice the size of the Social InSecurity alternative. What does this mean? It means that if 2000-2049 is as grim as 1900-1949, the proposed privatization plan is still twice as good as our current Social InSecurity abomination.

COMMENT	DATE	ACTUAL SS PAYROLL TAX	COMPOUND AT:	PAYOUT IN:	PRIVATE PENSION; APROX ANNUAL AMT
	1955	$100	11.5%	1997	$13,000
Prior to '55	'56	100	11.5	1998	13,000
SS taxes added	'57	100	11.7	1999	13,000
To '55-'58 to	'58	100	12.2	2000	13.000
Equal $100/yr	'59	120	11.6	'01	15,000
	'60	150	11.6	'02	18,000
S & P 500 index	'61	150	11.9	'03	18,000
Fund used for	'62	150	11.5	'04	18,000
investment	'63	175	12.2	'05	22,000
1955-1967:	'64	175	11.3	'06	22,000
Investments	'65	175	11.7	'07	22,000
Compounded	'66	275	11.7	'08	35,000
at 12%	'67	290	11.7	'09	37,000
IDS New	'68	300	13.0	'10	60,000
Dimensions	'69	350	12.9	'11	65,000
Mutual Fund	'70	350	13.9	'12	90,000
used for	'71	375	15.4	'13	110,000
investment	'72	400	14.3	'14	100,000
1968-1995	'73	550	13.8	'15	120,000
	'74	600	16.0	'16	240,000
After 1995 Funds	'75	700	18.9	'17	365,000
Compound at S&P	'76	750	18.5	'18	380,000
500 net rate for	'77	800	18.7	'19	520,000
1980-2000 (12%)	'78	1000	19.6	'20	780,000
	'79	1000	20.2	'21	845,000
	'80	1100	19.5	'22	850,000
	'81	1400	17.7	'23	560,000
	'82	1500	18.8	'24	600,000
	'83	1800	17.9	'25	720,000

	'84	2000	17.8	'26	670,000
	'85	2200	19.7	'27	700,000
	'86	2500	18.4	'28	680,000
	'87	2600	18.3	'29	665,000
	'88	2700	18.6	'30	690,000
	'89	2900	19.9	'31	800,000
	'90	3100	18.5	'32	740,000
				(I'm 100!)	
	'91	3200	20.5	'33	700,000
	'92	3300	16.1	'34	600,000
	'93	3400	18.4	'35	500,000
	'94	3600	19.5	'36	520,000
	'95	3600	28.0	'37	640,000
Start using 12%	'96	2000*	12.0	'38	250,000**
Net for all funds	'97	and every			and every year until
		Year thereafter			42 years after I die
		Until I die			
		*Roth IRA			**Tax Free!!

VI. The Retirement Certificate

If you've stayed with me this far, you must be sympathetic with many of my conclusions. You agree, I'm sure, that the 21st century will be at least a tad better than the 20th. I happen to think it will be immensely better, but no matter, a tad better suffices. You also realize that today's new-borns will easily reach 100 years, many will see 120 and some even 150. Most folks will still start thinking retirement around age 60 and will be retired by the 'new' retirement age of 67 or soon after. The popular SS 'solvency solution' of making people retire later and later on the grounds that increased longevity suggests that better health demands a longer work life (work is good –retirement means you're lazy). This may prove short-sighted. Technology may one day soon leave millions un—or under employed. We may want to encourage people to elect a new, non-paying career as early as possible. Our plan suggests that people should be able to retire whenever the mood strikes, as long as it's not before the magic age, 59.5.

We both recognize that today's retirement funding systems, public, private and personal are woefully inadequate for a new generation that plans to work for forty years and enjoy retirement for at least an additional 40 years. The public system, which we have dubbed 'Social InSecurity,' is actually counter productive. The corporate and personal retirement programs never contemplated a 40-year payment. You probably agree that the oft-stated goal of retiring at half your final salary is not particularly attractive. You also agree that retiring at two or three time your salary is much more worthy, although you are somewhat skeptical about your ability to achieve that goal. Finally, you are as skeptical as I about the commitment of our political leaders to truly correct the evils of the 'Social InSecurity' system. But, there is an answer, I feel, and it lies in a product that we'll call the Retirement Certificate.

The Retirement Certificate (RC) represents shares in a qualifying mutual fund. It is purchased in units of $500 or $1000 and looks very much like the detestable U.S. Savings Bond. It is purchased under Roth IRA rules and produces tax-free pay out on its maturity date. The maturity date is determined by the RC series. We'll primarily discuss the '66' series, which means the certificate matures 66 years from its date of issue.

Under SEC oversight, well respected mutual funds (let's say with a 10 year history and at least a three 'Morning-star' rating) will issue RC's on the first of each month, 12 times a year. As an example, we'll use my old favorite, the IDS New Dimensions Mutual fund, a solid performer for over thirty years. Now called American Express New Dimensions, the fund might issue its first series "66's" with the identifier AXP ND 012067. These would be sold on January 1, 2001 and would mature on January 1, 2067. Those sold on Feb.1, 2001 would be coded AXP ND 022067. Those sold in March of the following year would be coded AXP ND 032068 and so on.

There would be almost no circumstances under which the RC could be cashed in prior to maturity. Perhaps with a court order, if a life threatening illness demands major expenditures, but fundamentally, the RC's are designed to sit through the entire maturity cycle untouched and unchanged.

The RC's would be no-load and the fund manager would be allowed an expense ratio not to exceed 50% of that of the sponsoring fund. They would be sold in much the same manner as regular fund shares. There would be little, if any, communication between fund company and RC owner after the initial sale. No prospectuses, no proxy solicitations, no quarterly statements. Only an annual tax statement is required, although most RC's would be part of an IRA program.

RC's would, of course, have to survive SEC scrutiny and the fund companies must receive permission to jettison much of the non-productive paper work burden that hampers all funds. The sponsoring fund would maintain WEB sites showing daily closing values of each of the 12 issues each year of each series. Even though they can't be cashed in until maturity, people do like to see how they are doing.

The series '66' designed to mature in 66 years, is as you might have guessed, marketed to the newborn crowd. Once the public understands and appreciates the time value of money, particularly over a lifetime, it would seem that every parent and grandparent would want their new addition to have a RC. If past performance is any predictor, the RC owner is virtually guaranteed a rousing start for their retirement.

You may have heard of the famous Ibbotson Associates study that concluded that all stocks had grown 11.2% over the past 73 years. Not just the 500 'best' stocks like the S&P 500, but all stocks. Seventy-three years covers some of the worst market conditions imaginable. A horrific world war and an even more horrific (in economic terms) depression, and yet all stocks, winners and losers alike, returned, on average, 11.2%

Of course, as conventional thinking goes, no one buys an investment for 73 years. So it's all academic. Not any longer. Don't you think a well run mutual fund, evolving with the times (and better times, we like to think), could beat 11.2% over 73 years? And a 73 year RC, if you wanted one, would certainly be available.

Just how good would this $1000 RC be? Let's project the past 10, 20, 30 year performance of the IDS fund, plus the 10 and 20 year performance of the S & P 500, over the next 66 years and see what we get. We also have to estimate inflation over most of the 21st century. Three percent is consistent with recent history and seems about right. All numbers are approximations.

PAST PERFORMANCE		PROJECTED VALUE 2066 DOLLARS	PROJECTED VALUE 1999 DOLLARS
New D 10 year	20.0%	$260 million!!	$35 million!!
New D 20 year	20.2%	$260 million!!	$35 million!!
New D 30 year	13.0%	$ 4 million!!	$525,000
S & P 10 year	18.2 %	$100 million!!	$10 million!!
S & P 30 year	13.0%	$ 4 million!!	$525,000

Obviously, we can't use most of these numbers in an illustration. The 30 year numbers include some really bad years back in the 70's and are much more comfortable. Still a half million (constant) dollars isn't a bad way to kick off retirement. And if the 21st century is a bit better for us than the 20th was, a couple of percentage points improvement would move the constant dollar payoff to over $2 million. Furthermore, your RC will earn at least ½% more (lower expense ratio) a year more than its 'parent' and that adds up.

Think about it. You kick in $1000 as a christening present for the newborn child and you have pretty much guaranteed them several hundred thousand dollars as a retirement kick-off. And a good shot at several million. Is $1000 too rich for your blood? Go for the $500 RC. The payoff could still be well into six figures. Or get other relatives to kick in toward one of the $1000 RC's. Every newborn should have one. Think of it as a good luck charm, a hedge against whatever unknowns beset them in their senior years when you many not be around to help. And, whatever the outcome, it's all tax free.

There could, of course, be other RC denominations. A series 42 would be ideal for someone in their 20's who senses the need to put something away, no matter how painful. A $1000 series 42 RC each year suggests a pension of $125,000 a year starting 42 years after the first RC is purchased. A 36 year RC might well produce a $65,000 payoff. A person could plan an adequate and infinite retirement pay out properly using combinations of RC's.

That's the good news. The bad news is that RC's do not currently exist. It seems that they should, since the interests of all parties are congruent. The parent or grandparent wants an instrument that will grow optimally with almost no chance it will be cashed in prematurely. They know the young people believe in saving but never do it. Not only are they invincible but are equally confident that they will be wealthy some day and saving for retirement can certainly be put off until critical purchases (i.e. SUV) are paid for. (Did you know that over 50% of all job changes involve cashing in all or part of the job changers 401K?) And then it is too late for the 'time value of money' to show its muscle. To accommodate RC's, the Investment Act of 1940 might need a little updating, which, after 60 years might be viewed as a reasonable idea.

Procrastination is the deadliest enemy of the 'time value of money.' If you put off starting your retirement savings for a mere six years, you're likely to cut your eventual payoff (at 12%) in half. If you buy your grandchildren a $1000 RC at birth they could have a retirement nest egg (that they can't touch) of over $30,000 at age 24. Their business associates, also 24, who want to enjoy an equally comfortable retirement, but have no savings, would have to find and invest a $30,000 lump sum to catch up. How many 24 year olds have $30,000 lying around?

People of all ages can make good use of RC's to fill in the holes in their personal financial plan and to inexpensively hedge the possibility that they will be around for a piece of a second century. And of the many young people who think they will be rich someday, a few will realize that the easiest way to reach that goal is to buy an RC or two in their teens and early twenties.

The RC could be a boon to mutual fund companies. Fund companies are, by and large, bedeviled by turnover. People have a tendency, particularly with no-loads, to put money in, and then take it out long before the fund company collects enough expense fees to pay the acquisition costs. The current on-line trading binge has even affected mutual funds. The average holding period is now half what it was 10 years ago. The RC's acquisition costs can be amortized over the entire term 42, 66 or whatever number of years the series calls for. Even though their expense factors would be half that of the 'parent' fund, their profits, particularly in later years, would be significant. For example, if the parent fund maintains a 12% pace, the fund's total management fees over 66 years will approach $200,000, just for taking care of a $1000 investment.

You can, of course, create your own RC if the product doesn't become a reality. You won't get the very advantageous expense factor, of course, but you can insure that it won't be readily cashed in by setting up an 'education IRA' and/or trust much as we discussed in chapter III.

No, I haven't forgotten that IRA's are only for people with earned income. The only little children with earned income are the tots and toddlers that appear in TV commercials and movies. All of the illustrations that I have presented bring into sharp focus the incredible opportunity we have to change the retirement paradigm; to make people realize that a few tax sheltered dollars, invested on behalf of a very young person can go a long way toward solving two of our nations most vexing fiscal problems. The most obvious being the inability of the majority of our citizens to enjoy more than a bare bones, sustenance retirement. The second and far subtler problem is the widening gap between the rich and the poor. The rich are getting richer at an astonishing rate. And yes, there are more and more of them. But the ranks of the poor are growing even faster. They are improving their lot, but at a tortuous pace. Did you know that in the last decade the 'affluent' income grew 15%, the 'poor' income only 1%?

I can take you to places in this world where people of means live in armed encampments, forever threatened by the desperate masses around them. This is no way to live. But if someday every person perseveres, no matter how bleak his/her station, with the knowledge that when they retire they will have a 'fortune' waiting for them this could go a long way toward balancing the scales. The first step is a 'children's retirement IRA' law enacted by Congress.

An even better solution would be some form of privatization of the present 'Social InSecurity' system. Diverting some portion, or the first $1000, of payroll taxes to an investment fund would solve many of our retirement problems, particularly if personal funds could be added to the Social Security investment account.

Have you ever tried to visualize the future? In some detail? I often try, but usually get boggled. Let's try a scenario for 2070.

Let's suppose that our society has endorsed the concept that every child deserves to have a comfortable old age. It becomes a cultural norm that every child, no matter how wretched their circumstance, how destitute their parent(s), deserves to have a Retirement Certificate in their name at birth. Of the approximately four million babies born in the USA each year, probably 75% would receive their RC from their parents, grandparents and extended families. Our culture encourages even relatively poor families to pour thousands into showcase weddings for their offspring. If a RC at birth becomes the cultural norm, families will scramble to find the $1000 (or at least $500) to fund the RC. Family planning for young couples would include accounting for the necessary $1000 investment before deciding to have a baby. But, for maybe 25% of newborns not even $500 can be found to invest in their behalf. What better place for the current visionary, new money charity trusts like the Bill and Warren Foundation to effectively dispense their largesse? The Gates Family Trust could probably underwrite a million babies a year by itself with matching funds or outright gifts to those in need. Let's envision a nation where all children are prepared for retirement, one way or another, even before they attend pre-school. Then fast forward to 2070.

Every person, on his or her sixty-seventh birthday would find an Ed McMahon type at the door with a check. A check for something between 4 and 8 million dollars. It's like everyone wins the lottery. But it's much better than the lottery; it's totally tax-free. And it could happen again. To themselves, to their spouse, depending on decisions made some 66 years before.

What a wonderful world it would be! Wouldn't it? No more 'over the hill to the poorhouse,' no more parents moving in with the kids, no more despair, no more eating cat food, or just giving up. Try to think of the consequences. Most old people would be very comfortable.

Sure, I know that an average new car will cost over $50,000 in 2070 but $4 million is still a lot of money. Most of these folks will have their jobs, pensions, savings, Social Security—or will they? None of us can really anticipate what it would really be like. But wouldn't you like to give it a try?

Retirement in the 21st century will certainly be dramatically different than the 20th century retirement envisioned by our legislators in 1935 and by our government and employers in the decades that follow. There is much talk about the current prosperity being disproportionately enjoyed by the wealthy. This need not be. Nor need it be in the even greater prosperity of the 21st century. But it will take considerable energy, vision and determination by our leaders to make sure that all citizens enjoy the long, healthy and comfortable retirement that this book has demonstrated, we hope, can so readily be achieved.

VII. A Social Security Reform Proposal

The Perry Reform Plan

In 1977, the Advisory Council on Social Security proposed three separate plans for extending solvency for at least the next 75 years. I would like to suggest a fourth plan and then compare it to the other three. The Perry Plan has the following basis tenets:

A. Absolutely no (negative) changes to present participants. No reduction in disability benefits, no reduction in current pension payments, no reduction in dependent and survivor disability provisions.

B. In 1935 and throughout the first half of the 20th century, a guaranteed insurance system was highly desirable. But in the late 20th century, we became a nation of capital formation, investment and risk management. Ordinary Life Insurance is no longer relevant as a savings vehicle; insured pensions are an equally anachronistic foundation for retirement planning.

C. A guaranteed pension is not a constitutional right. But all citizens, no matter how modest their income should have the opportunity to retire at twice (or more) their working income. Today's Social Security system effectively prevents the marginal worker from achieving this goal. Government systems, without delving into means testing or welfare, should be biased toward the poorer worker; yet should give positive assistance to all workers in achieving the "twice or more" goal. The Perry System would work as follows:

All new entrants into the Social Security system would participate in an investment based, privatized pension system. Present participants in the SS system will be given an option to join the new system. [It might be feasible to even allow new entrants the option of joining. If the option were available for the first few years it could stop the opposition in its tracks.] They will be subject to age based limitations/incentives as described below. The maximum salary subject to payroll taxes would grow slowly to accommodate COLA (cost of living) increases to current retirees. The Perry System anticipates no change in the current payroll tax rate (6.2% for SS—plus 1.45% for Medicare with no cap).

The first $1000 of a participating worker's payroll tax will be earmarked for investment. The investment can be made in a 'Roth' mode or 'Regular IRA' mode. The participant will have the option of selecting the mode and periodically switching modes, but at most, once a year. In the 'Roth' option, the $1000 of payroll tax becomes taxable as income in the current year; the 'redemption' of that investment during retirement is tax-free. In the 'regular IRA' option, of course, the payroll tax is not considered income, but the eventual pay out would be fully taxable (some IRA rules, like the one requiring earned income, would have to change).

At the end of each year active participants (i.e. those with an investment balance) would be sent a statement showing investment status, inception to date, plus the amount of payroll taxes credited for investment in the year just completed. If the tax amount is less than $1000, the participant will be encouraged to 'make up the difference' so that a retirement investment can be made. Participants will also be encouraged to invest beyond the initial $1000, in increments of $1000, limited by the particular IRA rules that are appropriate. There will, however be absolutely no restrictions based on salary or age of the participant. The first $1000 collected by SSI (through taxes and/or contributions) will be invested in a $1000 Retirement Certificate (see chap. VI) maturing in the participant's 67th year. Any supplemental contributions in $1000 increments that year will be used to purchase additional certificates for that same 67th year. Miscellaneous balances would be rolled over to the following year. The next time $1000 is accumulated, it will be invested in the next open retirement year, in this case, the participants 68th year. The SSA will maintain a money market account for the participant and accept random deposits. Retirement Certificates would be designed to mature in the appropriate year assuming an initial retirement age of 67. Early retirement is possible with Retirement Certificates being redeemable after age 59.5, per IRA rules. It is imperative, however, that the RC is in force for a minimum of 36 years.

Savvy parents (parents will be soundly encouraged to become savvy) will see the wisdom in attaching a $1000 check to the request for their newborn's social security number. This alone gives the participant a huge jump-start in retirement; $1000 at birth could grow into several million dollars in 67 years. This could have enormous social benefit. Young people with a social services bent could be encouraged to follow a career as a Salvation Army professional (or whatever) without worrying about saving for retirement if their parents put a 'thou' or two in their SS kitty during the early years. Similarly, parents who would like their child to obtain a PHD in ancient Egyptian culture and become a teacher or curator could help immensely by making retirement contributions early on to cover the years that the child remains in school. One of the ironies of this system is that young people who are not 'college material' and start full time jobs at age 18 are in better retirement planning shape than their 'professional student' counterparts who manage to stay in school until they are 30. The parent (or grandparent) that puts $1000 to work at their child's birth can breathe easier, knowing that if all the child aspires to is to be an A & P bagboy (or girl) by day and a poet by night, their golden years will still be pretty darn good.

New participants in the Social Security system will have no guarantees of any basic pension. They are trading their minimum guarantee of today's system for an opportunity to have a pension 10 times as large (or even more) than the current system produces. They will 'outperform' Social Security unless securities over the next 50 years compound at less than 4% a year. The problem of including existing participants in Social Security is a bit more complex. Those under 30 years old are not much of a problem. Their Retirement Certificates will reach at least the minimum 36 years before normal retirement. They probably should be compensated for giving up their right to a traditional pension. Perhaps a slightly higher amount (over $1000) for each year in the current system would be fair. Participation would, of course, be strictly optional and no one ever loses his or her rights to disability and survivor benefits. Persons over 40 have a different problem. They cannot buy certificates that mature prior to their 76th birthday. They certainly should have the option of participating at a reduced guaranteed Social Security pension and/or have more than the basic first $1000 of payroll taxes be directed toward the privatized system. Better still might be a formula for giving current participants credit for full retirement at their SS pension rate but for a limited number of years. For example, a 30-year-old, working since age 20 might get five years retirement from SSA. Thus her contributions could be earmarked for her 72nd year and beyond; Social Security would pay normal retirement benefits for years 67—71. Similarly, a 40-year-old working since age 22 might get 9 years credit, allowing them to invest for ages 76 and beyond. The examples we have chosen give the new system enrollee at least 36 years for their RC's to mature. Thirty-six years should beat Social InSecurity even if equities return as little as 6% a year.

Retirement Certificates can only be issued by approved growth equity funds that meet minimum criteria (10 years solid history, 3 star rating, for example). The danger in privatization is not that unwary participants will invest in high-risk schemes but that they will invest in low risk products that cannot significantly out perform the current system. Abjectly risk averse persons would be allowed, after the 36-year minimum, to convert certificates to an appropriate bond fund without triggering the retirement process. The system requires no investment expertise, as all options are considered roughly equal. Participants would be allowed to choose, prior to April 15 of each year, a new mutual fund if they wish, and to switch from one IRA mode to the other. A whole new industry may emerge; predicting which mutual funds will perform best in the new year.

Do you think that those 'mean old' Wall St. types will make too much money? Then consider this. SSA could lower the expense bar. SSA could decree a sliding expense scale as a function of the length of time that a given investment must remain undisturbed. That is, a RC bought at birth cannot be redeemed for about 60 years; it might be allowed only a ½% expense factor. This could increase the shareholders 'take' by as much as 1.5%, a very significant sum over 60 years. A minimum RC (36 years) might be allowed a 1% expense factor. The fund companies will still do fine. Remember that since most of their portfolios cannot be redeemed or switched, they can invest without worrying about panicky shareholders cashing in at the slightest 'bear' tremor.

If a participant dies prematurely, the investment funds become a restricted part of the participant's estate. Certificates can only be redeemed after they reach 36 years. They are not designed to support a young widow, for example. The current survivor's system would attempt to meet this need, in the traditional fashion. The heir(s) would own the funds that would continue to grow. If the funds were substantial and the current need significant, the heirs could borrow against the eventual redemption through a process somewhat similar to that utilized in reverse mortgages. As you will recall, older people that live in valuable properties but have insufficient cash flow can secure a reverse mortgage against their property. In precisely the reverse of a conventional mortgage they receive a monthly check during the term of the mortgage. At the end of the mortgage term, the lender owns the house.

The SSA's long term pension liabilities will be drastically reduced. In the short term however, the trust fund will cease to grow and will erode to zero somewhat before the currently predicted 2029. If most people under forty opt out of the present system, there will be very few people retiring after 2029. There are two ways to maintain trust fund solvency. One is simply to use general revenues to shore up the trust fund. It is far more productive than using budget surplus funds to chip away at the National debt. A better way, however, would be to amortize the excessive early costs over the entire 80 years or so before SSA is completely out of the insured pension business. Tax rates could be kept constant throughout the 80 years, with deficits met by borrowing against future tax revenues. The amounts needed can rather easily be computed with considerable actuarial accuracy. The only variable might be how many pensioners live considerably longer than predicted. Young people, we are told, are those most disaffected with the present system. They also tend to be risk takers. If they support a new system such as we have described, the SSA should be able to predict exactly how much they need to gradually exit the pension business and determine when taxes can be reduced and/or investment amounts raised. What is imperative is that the low wage earner effectively invests a much higher percent of his/her payroll tax than does the person earning several times as much.

Comparison of Reform Plans (see chart on page 123)

Retirement Age: The Perry plan looks best. New entrants can retire when they please, as long as they are at least 59.5 years old and their initial investment has 'marinated' at least 36 years. Existing SS participants would have an option to join. If they do so, they would get a standard SS pension, at current retirement age, for a limited number of years.

Reduction of Benefits: Ball Plan leaves all benefits as they now are. The Perry plan provides no insured pension for new entrants, replacing that with a substantial investment opportunity. Optional participants lose some pension rights in return for investment participation. No one loses any non-pension benefits. The other two plans substantially reduce benefits.

Invest Trust Fund in Stocks: Perry plan lukewarm, others will consider. *Tax Implication*: Perry plan amortizes cost over 80 years when SSA pensions cease to exist. All others raise taxes and confront the problem again in 2075.

Investment/Savings Accounts: Perry plan produces ½ to 1% higher returns for approved investment funds and doesn't allow workers to make naïve investments. Optional additional investments could produce much higher total return than the next best plan (PSA). The Gamlich plan produces very modest savings accounts—only the maximum $60,000 earner saves as much as $1000 a year.

Investment Sophistication: Both Gamlich and Perry control options, reducing investment knowledge requirement significantly. But if Gamlish offers both fixed and equity investments, workers could make poor choices.

Fairness: All Advisory Council plans remain as regressive as the current system. The Perry approach reflects the belief that Social Security should be primarily for the people below the median income level. Those above the median have many options for supplemental pension funds. The Perry plan is particularly kind to the lower half of the lower half—those who have few if any options for building retirement dollars. Under the Perry plan, the $15,000 worker will save $1,000 a year, the same worker under PSA would save $750 and the under IA, only $240. Under the Perry plan the $15,000 worker would save as much toward retirement as would the $1,500,000 worker. This is as it should be.

Problem Solved?

Perry plan—Yes, forever
Ball plan—deferred until 2075, then rears its ugly head again.
Gamlish plan—same as Ball
PSA plan—same as Ball

The Privatization Wars

After reading this book could you imagine anyone being against privatization? I couldn't. Well, we're both wrong. They're coming out of the woodwork and they are adamant. The CATO Institute, a libertarian think tank, leads the proponents of privatization. Other support seems to come mostly from Republicans. It's enough to make anyone suspicious. CATO presents their arguments logically and unemotionally. The opponents, however, feel no such encumbrance. In all fairness, the most publicized privatization schemes contain some element of benefits reduction to make the numbers work. That's pretty scary.

AARP leads the charge by claiming there's nothing really wrong with Social Security, it won't go bankrupt. There's a little bit of ostrich in all of us, but solvency isn't the real issue. The real issue, as we continually point out, is the dreadfully inadequate pension produced by the present system. It seems strange that all the organizations devoted to the poor and voiceless-who are held in economic slavery by the present system— are lined up solidly against privatization. Characterizing the proponents as 'privateers' (read, pirates) they see Wall St. money behind every move. I never thought I'd be identified with those so villainous. [Year's ago we developed a market newsletter for our clients. We purposely named it "West of Wall St." to clearly distance ourselves from those miscreants.] There is, no doubt, considerable money being contributed by 'Wall St.' to further the cause of privatization.

Perhaps the saddest case is the position taken by the American Association of University Women. They rightfully point out that women earn less than men, have fewer years in the workforce to earn pension credits, receive less in private pensions ($2500 average vs. >$5000), and live longer to enjoy the largesse of Social Security. They wrongfully insist that the present system be kept intact to protect those women who are alone and would otherwise sink into poverty. Let's look at it logically. The single woman retires with a lower Social Security benefit than the average (which is $800) and has, on average, a $200 a month private pension. Give her $600 a month from SS plus her $200 company pension and she'd is lucky to break $10,000 a year. She must be treading water furiously to avoid sinking further into poverty.

Another stalwart from the loyal opposition claims that stocks will net only 2% over the next 25 years. Seems that historically equities have returned 7% (net of inflation) over the long haul. Since securities have earned 12% over the past 25 years, they must drop to 2% over the next 25 to bring the average back to par.

Makes sense? Yes? No! As far as I know there is no 11th Commandment that says "thou shalt make only 7% on equities." Nor is there any immutable law of physics that applies. The market has no life of its own; it simply reflects the economic situation and the outlook of investors involved. For centuries the economy staggered slowly upward, four steps forward, three steps back. Cotton Mather earned 7% on his portfolio in 1840; Sanford White did similarly at the turn of the century, as did 'wrong way' Roy Reigels in the roaring 20's, and Prof. Irwin Corey in the 60's. But that has little to do with today.

Another denizen of the dismal claims SS will outperform the stock market over the next 50 years because stocks will lose 75% of their value and corporate bonds will produce a negative real rate of return. How does he know this? I have no idea. But if these gentlemen of gloom are right it will be economic Armageddon and Social Security benefits will be the least of our problems. If this happens, we'll be better served if they put all us old geezers on our individual ice floes and push us gently out to sea. Then our offspring, like the fabled Eskimos of yore, can go back to their igloos to plan the hunt for the next meal.

The system we propose tries to meet these objections and construct an approach to privatization that everyone can embrace. Let's recap the highlights:

1.   Absolutely no reduction of benefits for present participants. No new taxes, no increase in retirement age.

2. Completely optional for present FICA taxpayers; new partici-
    pants have no guaranteed minimum pension. All other benefits
    remain without change. [As noted, participation might be
    optional for new participants as well. This needs considerable
    additional study.]
3. First $1000 in FICA taxes for all participants directed to private
    account and invested in qualifying equity mutual fund.
4. Voluntary contributions to private accounts encouraged; par-
    ents can assure a decent retirement for their child by contributing
    $1000 to child's SS account.
5. Poorer workers build retirement account as fast as richest worker
    (ignoring voluntary contributions); SS no longer regressive.
6. Specific retirement year investing suggests major death benefit
    for heirs. All will benefit, but poor people, who statistically don't
    live as long as the rich, gain the most.
7. "Wall Street" expenses capped at ½-1%, substantially reducing
    their profits. [If someone does something for us, but gets rich in
    the process, we detest them. It's the American way.]
8. Participants earn up to 1.5% more on their mutual funds than
    do the holders of comparable 'public' funds.
9. Full retirement available at age 60 for participants.
10. Roth IRA option allows tax-free retirement income for
    participants.
11. Specific retirement year investing allows 'time value of money' to
    optimize at up to 60 years 'marinating' for each year's
    contribution.
12. Volunteer contribution allows 'untouchable' retirement savings
    at better rates than comparable public funds

Comparison of Social Security Reform Plans

	Maintain Benefits Ball Plan	Individual Acct Gramlich Plan	Personal Security PSA	Maximum Security Perry Plan
Retirement age	Normal—67 Early—62	Normal—67 Early—62	Normal— 67 Early—62	New SS registrants: optional After 59.5. Others same as Ball
Will increase periodically?	Yes	Yes	Scheduled increases	No (new entrants)
Tax increase?	.8% + .8% effective 2045	1.6% employee only	1.52% (for 72 years)	None
Invest trust fund in *Stock market?*	Further study	Further study	Further study	Negative
Savings account?	No	Yes	Yes	Yes
Amount Saved	NA	1.6% of salary	5% of salary	1st $1000 of payroll tax
Investments available	NA	Limited and controlled	Any—employee option	Limited to approved
Disposition of funds at retirement	NA	Annuitized	Lump sum or annuity	Equity mutual funds Each year's cash released at certificate maturity
Disposition of funds at death	NA	Worker's estate	Worker's estate	Worker's estate after 36 Years for each investment
Additional Investment option?	NA	No	No	Yes—within IRA rules
Pension taxable?	Presume current, up to 85%	85% taxable (?)	85% taxable (?)	Roth option—not taxable Reg. IRA " 100% taxable
FICA tax cuts?	Never	Never	Never	Worst case—reduced 40% Employer & employee by 2075
Benefits reduced	No	Average 17%—all benefits at age 62 reduced over time	Flat Pension $410Mo. For full employment disability/survivor gradually reduced 33%	New—no pension Optional—limited full pension No reduction— disability/survivor
SSA solvent until...	2075	2075	2075	Infinity

VIII. Catastropic Health Care

The Problem

There's no question that living 'forever' implies serious health care costs, and if we successfully routinize transplant surgery, something beyond major medical insurance is needed. What we are looking for is something to take the pressure off health insurance, contribute significantly to easing the Medicare dilemma, and, finally, to pay for the sort of draconian procedures that are often the subject of media coverage. Invariably in these cases the HMO refuses to pay hundreds of thousands of dollars (if not millions) for a controversial life saving procedure and the unfortunate victim dies.

The product I'm envisioning probably requires a public/private partnership, as it would involve setting up reserves that wouldn't be validated for 50 years or more.

This subject is worthy of extensive research, perhaps even a book of its own, but I believe the concepts presented herein have substantial potential. If the solution isn't precisely as I've described, a variation on the theme might well solve the problem of rising health care costs, particularly for the elderly.

There are several issues confronting us:

1. Heath care costs continue to rise. Managed Care providers and HMO's are under great pressure to improve their 'bedside manner' and approve benefits more liberally.
2. Medicare continues to do less and cost more. Anita and I both pay Medicare a $41 monthly premium as well as paying Aetna $200 a month for a heavily subsidized supplemental coverage

plan. In the early 60's my company fought bitterly against the original Medicare bill; we thought private insurance would prevail. Can you imagine where the $180 billion that Medicare spends annually would come from?

3.   Civic leaders are beginning to talk about rationing health care. One western governor suggested that an 80-year-old who wanted a heart transplant should not be allowed to have one, even if he had the money to pay for it. Too many accept this premise as being unfortunate but inevitable.

4.   Coverage is being denied for extreme procedures as described above.

5.   By the time the need is recognized, nursing home premiums are beyond the reach of most seniors. Without insurance, a Medicaid nursing home stay can be grim.

Catastrophic Health Care

PREMIUMS: The answer to many of our health care cost concerns might be in a product that I like to call Catastrophic Health Care (CHC). CHC would be sold on a single lifetime premium basis to persons with no major pre-existing conditions as follows:

Age of Insured	Premium
0–6 months	$250
6 months–12 years	additional $25 for each 6 months
12–25 years	additional $50 for each 6 months

COVERAGE: CHC is a super major medical policy that pays for all major illnesses, operations, procedures, etc. after a $50,000 deductible. An independent advisory board of prominent physicians and civilians would determine whether an experimental or controversial treatment is covered. The decision would be made without undue consideration of the impact on the reserves from which the claims would be paid.

When hardship can be demonstrated, the policy would have, in effect, a disappearing deductible. That is, a person that couldn't afford, or didn't have access to private health insurance could have full coverage for catastrophic illnesses where costs exceed $50,000.

ADMINISTRATION: The program would be overseen by the Social Security Administration. All newborn babies would be issued a Social Security number and every effort would be made to assure that each newborn becomes a policyholder. It would be easy, but probably not wise, to have the Federal Government pay these premiums. With nearly four million youngsters born annually the cost would be 'only' $1 billion. A better approach might be a high tax deduction (perhaps near 100%), intensive social agency promotion, and private contributions to cover any child too poor or too neglected, that might 'fall through the cracks.'

TRUST FUND: All premiums would be paid into a trust fund designed solely for the benefit of the children enrolled in that specific year. If, each year, 4 million (give or take) children were enrolled, approximately $1 billion would be paid into the trust. At the end of the year the trust would be closed and would receive only investment income thereafter. The first fund, Trust 2000, would benefit enrolled children born in 2000 until all enrollees die or the fund is depleted. Trust fund 2001 would start at the real millennium and enroll children born in 2001 until year-end, raising its billion-dollar 'endowment.' And so on, year after year. Trusts would also be set up for years prior to 2000, to accommodate children born as early as 1975, perhaps.

TRUST FUND MANAGEMENT: SSA would accept bids from major investment firms to manage the fund's portfolio. It should be a high prestige assignment and a unique opportunity to 'run' a billion dollars for 60 or more years with little 'redemption' or other disturbance. The selected money manager would be instructed to maximize returns over the first 60 years and would be well compensated for outperforming comparable fund managers but poorly compensated for lack-luster performance. Only minimal expenses would be allowed.

CLAIM PAYMENT: Medicare might administer claim payment but would not be involved in determining claim validity in controversial cases. During the first 50 years there should not be many catastrophic illnesses; perhaps .3% of the policyholders would suffer beyond the $50,000 deductible. Even if the claims were to be on average $200,000, the total claim pay out would 'only' be $2-3 billion over the 50-year buildup. We say 'only' because of the funds investment potential.

INVESTMENT PERFORMANCE: Our long term target for each trust is 12% annual growth. We will assume a 4% inflation factor, since medical costs tend to rise faster than the CPI. Our 8% net growth is quite modest; most money managers think the can produce 12%, net, in their sleep. In any event, at 8% net the trust will make seven turns before any of the 'millenium' babies reaches Medicare eligibility. If you're keeping score, that's 128 billion dollars! You don't want to know what it would be if they actually achieved 12%. [It'd be almost a trillion dollars.] Sure, there'd be many more claims when the youngsters are 50-65 years old, but we can easily withstand a billion dollars or two each year. After 65 years have past, Trust Fund 2000 has $100 billion or so in reserves and about 3.2 million constituents (only about 20% will die before reaching retirement age).

ELDERLY HEALTH CARE: With a most conservative scenario, we end up with our initial group of insureds owning a trust that contains over $100 billion in constant dollars, and is still earning 12% on its reserves. Could it take over all health care (including all reasonable nursing home costs, with no time limit) for its three million or so 'owners?' I would certainly think so. Even a poorly performing trust should be able to pay its constituents' Medicare supplemental premiums. Moreover, since the fund pays for all catastrophic claims over $50,000, regular health insurance premiums can be reduced appropriately throughout the insured's lifetime. It may not be much, but every little bit helps. And then again, it may be substantial.

Each year will produce a new trust, and each year's babies will benefit in their old age to the extent their trust is well managed. Think of the potential. Currently Medicare spends upward of $200 billion a year for all 'blue hairs' and 'gray beards' and has reserves of $150 billion. In our scenario, each year, each new group of 65 year-olds brings $100 billion with them. Couldn't this mean the end of the Medicare problem?

CONCLUSION: Having the Medicare 'problem' cured by 2065 may not be soon enough for some people. For the impatient, it is feasible to construct trust funds for the children of the '80's & '90's. The initial premium must be considerably higher to offset the time loss that the 'time value of money' so earnestly covets. Using an 8% growth factor, the '90's child should pay, on a scaled basis, up to $500 (the amount $250 would become, compounding for 9 years) and the '80's children up to about $1500. These amounts are not onerous and additional tax incentives might make them more palatable. Since going 'backwards' requires no inflation adjustment, we might be able to accommodate 1975's 'child', by delaying the transition until the fund has adequate reserves. If successful, this effort could produce measurable relief to the health care system in the 2040's. One could build a case for going back as far as 1964 (sorry, no 'baby boomers' allowed).

What Is Prosperity?

Whatever it is we've had a lot of it for the past 10 years or so. Technical definitions aside, it seems to mean that 'everyone' who wants a job has one, and we all seem to have a least a little more money than last year. Maybe 10% of us have a lot more money than we used to have, and most of the wealth seems to come from the stock market. But only 25% of us own stocks (outside our 401K's) and about half of all families have less than $1000 in tangible net worth.

Prosperity has meant annual gains in productivity of 3-4%, with inflation consistently below 3%. Let's suppose that this continues on indefinitely. On a year to year basis it's not so extraordinary and perhaps the wise men of Washington have learned how to harness an economy that wants to explode to 10% growth per year until it collapses, and make it content with 3%, indefinitely.

As the years roll by, 30, 40, 50, the rich move from 2% to maybe 4-5% of the population, perhaps 40% of us own stocks, and only 30% of families have less than $1000 in tangible net worth. Hardly universal prosperity, but certainly an improvement.

Let us suppose we had the foresight to make sure that every child of the Millennium was gifted at birth with $1000 for their old age pension and $250 for their eventual elder health care. And let's agree that SSA administers these programs that allow individual contributions to their pensions and earmarks the first $1000 of each worker's FICA taxes for equity investment.

And as our millennium babies (and some pre-2000 babies that we grandfathers have succeeded in 'grandfathering') reach retirement age, they are incredibly blessed. Thy will receive an enormous tax-free retirement check plus a pension several times their previous salary, as well as free lifetime medical care without conditions or onerous co-payments. The new seniors will all own equities and have a tangible net worth that moves them into the top 10%, with incomes far above the previous median.

But tarry a moment. Let us suppose that even with all the retirement reforms we've described, the first half of the new century turns out to be fairly mediocre. Not nearly as good as the 90's, it rather mirrors the last 75 years of the 20th century. I can give no good reason why, but it is not impossible. How do our Millennium babies fare? Well, the 'time value of money' has to work harder, but even mediocre equity performance is still better than any alternative. Our Millennium baby's retirement will get started with a very substantial tax-free lump sum, enough for most people to live adequately on the income alone. But they will also get a 'new' Social Security pension that's about four times as good as the old SS program, is probably totally tax-free and, in case of premature demise, provides their heirs with a significant income. They will also have their Medicare and supplemental policy premiums paid for.

Think about it. Prosperous half century or mediocre 50 years, the 'new' seniors will be comfortable for life, and a long happy life it will be. Everyone will share in whatever level of prosperity we achieve. There is no downside for the reform plans we suggest, it's a win-win for all.

About the Author

George M. Perry was born in New London, Ct. He graduated from Tufts University in 1954 and joined the Travelers Insurance Co. as one of the nation's first computer programmers. He was appointed 2nd Vice President in 1968. He left the Travelers in 1970 to start Datagraphics, Inc., a cutting edge firm in computerized typesetting. George became Vice-President of data processing for the Home Insurance Co. in 1972. During his tenure at the Home, he was very active in several industry associations and was instrumental in establishing the agent/ company research organization now called 'ACCORD.'

In 1979, Perry moved to Minneapolis to become VP of Information Systems for Investors Diversified Services which is now American Express Financial Advisors. In the last dozen years of his career, as VP for Strategy and Development, he set up several new businesses that are now an integral part of American Express. He retired in 1995 and presently serves on the board of American Express Insurance Co., and is Chairman of the Board of iPOOL Inc., an Internet startup. George and his wife, Anita have three children and seven grandchildren. An avid bridge player, he is currently a bronze Life Master. He and Anita enjoy adventure travel which has provided them with many a fascinating experience in far reaches of the globe. They presently reside in Old Lyme, Ct. and maintain an apartment in New York City.

Appendix

The triangular arrays included in this appendix are the CPI (inflation), the S&P 500 index, both from 1956 to 1997, as well as two well-known equity mutual funds. The Equity Growth Fund 'A' is shown from its inception in 1968 to 1997, and the Equity Growth Fund 'B' is similarly shown from 1972 to 1997.

I used similar charts during my working years and have found them to be fascinating and illuminating. I hope you find them useful.

How to read the triangular arrays

Here's an example of an array (read from right to left):

Beginning investment year

	1995	1996	1997
1995	7.6%		
1996	8.6%	10.1%	
1997	6.3%	5.6%	1.3%

- The total return was 1.3% for 1997, 10.1% for 1996, and 7.7% for 1995
- A person investing in Jan. 1995 and holding the fund through 1997 would have received a three-year average annual total return of 6.3%.
- A person investing in January 1995 and holding the fund through 1996 would have received a two-year average annual total return of 8.8%.
- If using the CPI chart, the average inflation from 1995-1997 was 6.3%

EQUITY GROWTH FUND 'A'   INCEPTION 02/01/72
ANNUAL COMPOUNDED RATES OF RETURN

Year	1972	1973	1974	1975	1976	1977	1978	1979	1980	1981	1982	1983	1984	1985	1986	1987	1988	1989	1990	1991	1992	1993	1994	1995	1996	1997
1972	68.7																									
1973	11.7	-26.1																								
1974	-9.1	-33.2	-39.6																							
1975	-0.7	-16.7	-11.6	29.3																						
1976	2.8	-9.1	-2.6	23.6	18.2																					
1977	3.8	-5.8	0.1	18.5	13.5	8.9																				
1978	5.7	-2.2	3.5	18.4	14.9	13.3	17.9																			
1979	9.6	3.1	9.1	22.6	21.1	22.1	29.1	41.3																		
1980	15.6	10.3	16.8	30.3	30.5	33.8	43.3	58.1	76.8																	
1981	14.7	9.9	15.5	26.7	26.3	28.1	33.2	38.8	37.5	7.1																
1982	16.3	12.1	17.3	27.5	27.2	28.8	33.2	37.3	35.9	19.2	32.8															
1983	16.1	12.1	16.9	25.8	25.4	26.5	29.7	32.1	29.9	17.3	22.8	13.5														
1984	12.9	9.2	13.1	20.5	19.7	21.3	21.9	18.4	7.1	7.1	7.1	-3.8	-18.5													
1985	14.4	11.1	14.9	21.8	21.1	21.4	23.1	23.9	21.2	12.3	13.7	8.1	5.3	36.2												
1986	14.8	11.7	15.3	21.6	21.1	21.2	22.7	23.3	20.9	13.5	14.9	10.8	9.9	27.6	19.5											
1987	13.7	10.8	14.1	19.7	19.1	19.1	20.1	20.3	17.9	11.3	12.1	8.3	7.1	17.2	8.8	-1.1										
1988	13.3	10.5	13.6	18.8	18.1	18.1	18.9	19.1	16.7	10.8	11.4	8.1	7.1	14.7	8.3	3.1	7.4									
1989	14.5	11.7	14.9	19.9	19.2	19.3	20.2	20.5	18.5	13.4	14.2	11.8	11.5	18.7	14.7	13.2	21.1	36.4								
1990	13.9	11.4	14.1	18.8	18.1	18.1	18.8	18.9	17.1	12.3	12.9	10.7	10.3	16.1	12.3	10.6	14.7	18.6	3.2							
1991	15.3	13.1	15.8	20.3	19.7	19.8	20.6	20.9	19.3	15.1	16.1	14.2	14.3	20.1	17.5	17.1	22.1	27.6	23.1	47.1						
1992	15.1	12.8	15.3	19.6	19.1	19.1	19.8	19.9	18.4	14.5	15.2	13.6	13.6	18.4	16.1	15.5	19.1	22.3	17.9	26.1	8.1					
1993	14.7	12.6	15.1	18.9	18.4	19.1	19.1	17.7	14.1	14.6	14.6	13.2	13.7	17.3	15.1	14.5	17.3	19.4	15.5	19.9	8.3	8.5				
1994	14.1	12.1	14.4	18.1	17.5	17.5	18.1	18.1	16.6	13.2	13.7	12.2	12.1	15.8	13.7	13.1	15.1	16.5	12.9	15.4	6.5	5.7	3.1			
1995	15.2	13.3	15.5	19.1	18.6	18.6	19.2	19.3	18.1	14.9	15.5	14.2	14.3	17.9	16.2	15.8	18.1	19.7	17.2	20.2	14.3	16.4	20.6	41.1		
1996	15.5	13.7	15.9	19.3	18.9	18.9	19.5	19.6	18.4	15.5	16.1	14.9	15.1	18.4	16.9	16.7	18.8	20.3	18.2	20.9	16.2	18.4	21.9	32.6	24.5	
1997	15.7	14.1	16.1	19.4	19.1	19.1	19.5	19.6	18.5	15.8	16.3	15.3	15.5	18.6	17.2	17.1	19.1	20.4	18.5	20.9	17.1	18.9	21.6	28.5	22.6	20.8

EQUITY GROWTH FUND 'B'   INCEPTION 07/01/68
ANNUALLY COMPOUNDED RATES OF RETURN

	1968	1969	1970	1971	1972	1973	1974	1975	1976	1977	1978	1979	1980	1981	1982	1983	1984	1985	1986	1987	1988	1989	1990	1991	1992	1993	1994	1995	1996	1997
1968	17.6																													
1969	1.3	-12.7																												
1970	-6.1	-16.1	-19.2																											
1971	5.3	1.6	9.5	48.5																										
1972	9.4	7.4	15.1	37.4	27.1																									
1973	1.9	-1.1	2.2	10.6	-4.6	-28.4																								
1974	-4.4	-7.6	-6.5	-3.1	-15.9	-31.6	-34.7																							
1975	-0.8	-3.2	-1.5	2.5	-6.6	-15.7	-8.5	28.3																						
1976	0.8	-1.1	0.7	4.5	-2.6	-8.9	-1.3	21.3	14.7																					
1977	0.9	-0.8	0.8	4.1	-1.9	-6.9	0.5	14.5	8.1	1.9																				
1978	1.7	0.2	1.7	4.7	-0.4	-4.4	1.3	13.1	8.5	5.5	9.2																			
1979	4.1	2.8	4.5	7.6	3.3	0.3	6.1	16.9	14.3	14.1	20.7	33.5																		
1980	7.3	6.4	8.4	11.6	8.1	6	12.1	22.6	21.5	23.3	31.4	44.1	55.5																	
1981	6.8	6.1	7.7	10.5	7.3	5.3	10.5	19.2	17.7	18.3	22.8	27.7	24.9	0.4																
1982	8.4	7.7	9.5	12.3	9.5	7.9	12.9	20.9	19.9	20.7	24.9	29.2	27.8	15.8	33.6															
1983	9.1	8.5	10.2	12.9	10.3	8.9	13.6	20.8	19.9	20.7	24.1	27.3	25.8	17.2	26.7	20.1														
1984	8.2	7.7	9.2	11.5	9.1	7.7	11.8	18.1	16.9	17.2	19.5	21.3	19.1	11.4	15.3	7.1	-4.6													
1985	9.6	9.1	10.7	13.1	10.8	9.7	13.7	19.5	18.7	19.1	21.5	23.3	21.7	15.9	20.2	16.1	14.1	36.1												
1986	10.1	9.7	11.2	13.4	11.4	10.3	14.1	19.5	18.7	19.1	21.2	22.8	21.3	16.4	19.9	16.7	15.6	27.3	19.1											
1987	10.3	10.1	11.4	13.5	11.6	10.7	14.1	19.2	18.4	18.8	20.6	21.9	20.6	16.3	19.1	16.4	15.5	23.1	17.1	15.3										
1988	10.2	9.9	11.2	13.2	11.4	10.5	13.7	18.3	17.6	17.8	19.4	20.5	19.1	15.2	17.5	15.1	14.1	19.2	14.1	11.6	8.1									
1989	11.1	10.8	12.1	14.1	12.4	11.6	14.8	19.2	18.5	18.8	20.4	21.4	20.3	16.9	19.2	17.2	16.8	21.6	18.2	17.9	19.2	31.6								
1990	10.9	10.6	11.8	13.6	12.1	11.3	14.2	18.3	17.6	17.8	19.1	20.1	18.9	15.7	17.5	15.7	15.1	18.7	15.5	14.6	14.4	17.8	5.4							
1991	12.3	12.1	13.3	15.2	13.7	13.1	16.1	20.1	19.4	19.8	21.2	22.1	21.2	18.5	20.5	19.1	19.1	22.8	20.7	21.1	22.6	27.8	26.1	50.7						
1992	12.1	11.8	13.1	14.7	13.3	12.7	15.4	19.1	18.6	18.8	20.1	20.8	19.9	17.4	19.1	17.7	17.4	20.5	18.4	18.3	18.9	21.8	18.7	25.9	5.3					
1993	12.1	11.9	13.1	14.7	13.3	12.7	15.3	18.8	18.3	18.5	19.6	20.4	19.5	17.1	18.6	17.3	17.1	19.7	17.8	17.7	18.1	20.2	17.5	21.9	9.6	14.1				
1994	11.5	11.2	12.3	13.9	12.6	12.1	14.4	17.6	17.1	17.2	18.2	18.8	17.8	15.5	16.8	15.5	15.1	17.2	15.3	14.9	14.8	16.1	13.1	15.1	5.2	5.2	-3.1			
1995	12.3	12.1	13.1	14.7	13.5	12.9	15.3	18.4	17.9	18.1	19.1	19.7	18.9	16.7	18.1	16.9	16.7	18.8	17.2	17.1	17.2	18.6	16.6	18.9	12.1	14.5	14.7	35.6		
1996	12.7	12.5	13.5	15.1	13.9	13.4	15.6	18.7	18.2	18.4	19.4	20.1	19.2	17.2	18.5	17.4	17.2	19.3	17.8	17.7	18.1	19.3	17.7	19.8	14.5	16.9	17.8	29.9	24.4	
1997	13.1	12.9	13.9	15.4	14.3	13.8	16.1	18.9	18.5	18.7	19.6	20.2	19.5	17.7	18.8	17.9	17.8	19.7	18.3	18.4	18.6	19.9	18.5	20.5	16.1	18.4	19.5	28.1	24.5	24.6

S&P 500 (WITH DIVIDENDS) ANNUALLY COUMPOUNDED RATES OF RETURN

	1956	1957	1958	1959	1960	1961	1962	1963	1964	1965	1966	1967	1968	1969	1970	1971	1972	1973	1974	1975	1976	1977
1956	6.3																					
1957	-2.1	-9.8																				
1958	10.6	12.9	41.2																			
1959	10.8	12.4	25.5	11.5																		
1960	8.7	9.3	16.5	5.9	0.5																	
1961	11.5	12.6	19	12.5	12.9	26.9																
1962	8.4	8.8	12.9	6.8	5.2	7.7	-8.6															
1964	10.1	10.7	14.5	9.8	9.4	12.5	5.9	22.8														
1964	10.8	11.4	14.8	10.9	10.8	13.5	9.3	19.6	16.4													
1965	11.1	11.5	14.5	11.1	11.1	13.3	10.1	17.2	14.4	12.5												
1966	8.9	9.1	11.5	8.2	7.8	9.1	5.7	9.7	5.6	0.6	-10.1											
1967	10.1	10.4	12.6	9.9	9.7	11.1	8.6	12.4	9.9	7.8	5.6	23.9										
1968	10.1	10.5	12.5	10.1	9.8	11.1	8.9	12.2	10.2	8.6	7.4	17.3	11.1									
1969	8.7	8.9	10.6	8.2	7.8	8.7	6.6	9.1	6.8	5.1	3.2	8.1	0.9	-8.4								
1970	8.4	8.5	10.1	7.8	7.5	8.2	6.3	8.3	6.4	4.8	3.3	7.1	1.9	-2.4	3.9							
1971	8.7	8.9	10.4	8.3	8.1	8.7	7.1	9.1	7.3	6.1	5.1	8.4	4.8	2.8	8.9	14.2						
1972	9.3	9.5	10.9	9.1	8.8	9.5	8.1	9.9	8.6	7.6	7.1	10.1	7.5	6.6	12.2	16.5	18.9					
1973	7.8	7.9	9.1	7.2	6.9	7.5	6.1	7.4	6.1	4.9	4.1	6.1	3.4	2	4.7	5.1	0.7	-14.7				
1974	5.7	5.6	6.6	4.7	4.3	4.6	3.1	4.1	2.5	1.2	0.1	1.4	-1.5	-3.4	-2.4	-3.9	-9.3	-20.8	-26.4			
1975	7.1	7.1	8.1	6.4	6.1	6.5	5.2	6.3	5.1	4.1	3.3	4.9	2.7	1.5	3.3	3.2	0.6	-4.9	0.5	37.2		
1976	7.8	7.9	8.9	7.3	7.1	7.5	6.3	7.5	6.4	5.6	5.1	6.6	4.8	4.1	6.1	6.4	4.9	1.6	7.7	30.3	23.8	
1977	7.1	7.1	8.1	6.5	6.2	6.6	5.4	6.4	5.3	4.5	3.9	5.3	3.6	2.8	4.3	4.3	2.7	-0.2	3.8	16.4	7.2	-7.2
1978	7.1	7.1	7.9	6.5	6.3	6.6	5.5	6.4	5.4	4.7	4.1	5.4	3.8	3.1	4.5	4.6	3.3	0.9	4.3	13.9	7.1	-0.5
1979	7.5	7.5	8.4	7.1	6.8	7.2	6.2	7.1	6.2	5.6	5.1	6.3	5.1	4.5	5.8	6.1	5.1	3.3	6.6	14.8	9.8	5.5
1980	8.4	8.5	9.4	8.1	7.9	8.3	7.4	8.4	7.6	7.1	6.7	8.1	6.9	6.6	8.1	8.5	7.8	6.5	10.1	17.6	14.1	11.7
1981	7.9	7.9	8.7	7.5	7.3	7.7	6.8	7.7	6.9	6.3	6.1	7.1	6.1	5.6	6.9	7.2	6.5	5.2	8.1	14.1	10.6	8.1
1982	8.3	8.4	9.2	8.1	7.9	8.3	7.4	8.3	7.6	7.1	6.8	8.1	7.1	6.7	8.1	8.3	7.8	6.7	9.4	15.1	12.1	10.3
1983	8.8	8.9	9.7	8.6	8.5	8.8	8.1	8.9	8.3	7.9	7.6	8.8	7.9	7.7	8.9	9.3	8.9	8.1	10.7	15.8	13.4	11.9
1984	8.7	8.8	9.6	8.5	8.4	8.7	8.1	8.8	8.2	7.8	7.6	8.6	7.8	7.6	8.8	9.1	8.7	7.9	10.3	14.8	12.5	11.2
1985	9.4	9.5	10.3	9.3	9.2	9.6	8.9	9.7	9.2	8.8	8.7	9.7	9.1	8.9	10.1	10.5	10.2	9.6	11.9	16.2	14.3	13.3
1986	9.7	9.8	10.6	9.6	9.5	9.9	9.3	10.1	9.6	9.3	9.1	10.2	9.5	9.4	10.6	11.1	10.8	10.2	12.4	16.4	14.7	13.9
1987	9.6	9.7	10.4	9.5	9.4	9.7	9.1	9.9	9.4	9.1	8.9	9.9	9.3	9.2	10.3	10.6	10.4	9.9	11.9	15.5	13.9	13.1
1988	9.8	9.9	10.6	9.7	9.6	10.1	9.4	10.1	9.7	9.4	9.3	10.2	9.6	9.5	10.6	11.1	10.8	10.3	12.2	15.6	14.1	13.3
1989	10.4	10.5	11.2	10.3	10.3	10.6	10.1	10.9	10.4	10.2	10.1	11.1	10.5	10.5	11.5	12.1	11.8	11.4	13.3	16.6	15.3	14.6
1990	9.9	10.1	10.7	9.9	9.8	10.2	9.6	10.3	9.9	9.7	9.5	10.4	9.9	9.8	10.8	11.1	11.1	10.6	12.3	15.3	13.9	13.3
1991	10.5	10.6	11.3	10.5	10.4	10.8	10.3	11.1	10.6	10.4	10.3	11.2	10.7	10.7	11.6	12.1	11.9	11.5	13.2	16.1	14.9	14.3
1992	10.4	10.5	11.1	10.4	10.3	10.7	10.2	10.9	10.5	10.3	10.2	11.1	10.6	10.5	11.4	11.8	11.7	11.3	12.9	15.6	14.5	13.9
1993	10.4	10.5	11.1	110.4	10.3	10.6	10.2	10.8	10.5	10.3	10.2	11.1	10.5	10.5	11.4	11.7	11.6	11.3	12.8	15.3	14.2	13.7
1994	10.1	10.2	10.8	10.1	10.1	10.4	9.9	10.5	10.1	9.9	9.9	10.6	10.2	10.1	11.1	11.3	11.1	10.8	12.2	14.6	13.5	12.9
1995	10.8	10.9	11.5	10.8	10.7	11.1	10.6	11.3	10.9	10.7	10.7	11.5	11.1	11.1	11.9	12.2	12.1	11.8	13.2	15.6	14.6	14.1
1996	11.1	11.2	11.8	11.1	11.1	11.4	11.1	11.6	11.3	11.1	11.1	11.8	11.4	11.5	12.3	12.8	12.5	12.3	13.6	15.9	15.1	14.6
1997	11.5	11.7	12.2	11.6	11.6	11.9	11.5	12.2	11.9	11.7	11.7	12.5	12.1	12.2	13.1	13.3	13.3	13.1	14.4	16.6	15.6	15.4

1978 1979 1980 1981 1982 1983 1984 1985 1986 1987 1988 1989 1990 1991 1992 1993 1994 1995 1996 1997

6.6
12.4 18.6
18.8 25.4 32.5
12.3 14.3 12.3 -4.9
14.1 16.1 15.3 7.5 21.6
15.5 17.4 17.1 12.3 22.1 22.5
14.1 15.4 14.8 10.8 16.6 14.1 6.3
16.2 17.6 17.5 14.7 20.2 19.7 18.3 31.7
16.5 17.8 17.8 15.3 19.9 19.5 18.5 25.1 18.7
15.3 16.3 16.1 13.8 17.3 16.5 15.1 18.1 11.7 5.2
15.4 16.3 16.1 14.2 17.2 16.5 15.3 17.7 13.3 10.7 16.6
16.7 17.6 17.5 16.1 18.9 18.5 17.9 20.3 17.6 17.3 23.8 31.5
15.1 15.7 15.5 13.9 16.2 15.6 14.6 16.1 13.1 11.8 14.1 12.8 -3.2
16.1 16.8 16.7 15.3 17.6 17.1 16.5 18.1 15.9 15.3 18.1 18.4 12.4 30.5
15.5 16.1 15.9 14.7 16.6 16.1 15.4 16.6 14.6 14.1 15.8 15.6 10.8 18.5 7.6
15.1 15.7 15.5 14.3 16.1 15.6 14.9 15.9 14.1 13.4 14.8 14.5 19.6 15.6 8.8 10.1
14.3 14.8 14.5 13.3 14.9 14.3 13.6 14.4 12.6 11.8 12.8 12.2 8.7 11.9 6.3 5.6 1.3
15.4 16.1 15.8 14.8 16.3 16.1 15.4 16.3 14.8 14.4 15.6 15.5 13.1 16.6 13.4 15.3 18.1 37.6
15.8 16.4 16.2 15.3 16.8 16.4 16.1 16.8 15.6 15.3 16.4 16.4 14.4 17.6 15.2 17.2 19.7 30.1 23.1
16.6 17.2 17.1 16.3 17.7 17.5 17.1 18.1 17.1 16.8 18.1 18.2 16.6 19.8 18.1 20.3 23.1 31.2 28.1 33.4

CONSUMER PRICE INDEX ANNUAL COMPOUNDED RATES

	1956	1957	1958	1959	1960	1961	1962	1963	1964	1965	1966	1967	1968	1969	1970	1971	1972	1973	1974	1975	1976	1977
1956	2.9																					
1957	2.9	3.1																				
1958	2.6	2.4	1.8																			
1959	2.3	2.1	1.6	1.5																		
1960	2.1	1.9	1.6	1.4	1.4																	
1961	1.9	1.7	1.3	1.2	1.1	0.7																
1962	1.8	1.6	1.3	1.2	1.1	0.9	1.2															
1963	1.8	1.6	1.4	1.3	1.2	1.2	1.4	1.6														
1964	1.7	1.5	1.3	1.3	1.2	1.2	1.3	1.4	1.2													
1965	1.7	1.6	1.4	1.4	1.3	1.3	1.5	1.6	1.5	1.9												
1966	1.9	1.8	1.6	1.6	1.6	1.7	1.9	2.1	2.2	2.6	3.4											
1967	2.1	1.9	1.8	1.8	1.8	1.9	2.1	2.2	2.4	2.8	3.2	3.1										
1968	2.2	2.1	2.1	2.1	2.1	2.2	2.4	2.6	2.9	3.3	3.7	3.9	4.7									
1969	2.4	2.4	2.4	2.4	2.5	2.6	2.9	3.1	3.4	3.8	4.3	4.6	5.3	6.1								
1970	2.6	2.6	2.6	2.7	2.8	2.9	3.2	3.4	3.7	4.1	4.5	4.8	5.4	5.7	5.5							
1971	2.7	2.7	2.7	2.7	2.8	3.1	3.2	3.4	3.6	4.1	4.3	4.5	4.9	5.1	4.4	3.4						
1972	2.7	2.7	2.7	2.8	2.9	3.1	3.2	3.4	3.6	3.9	4.2	4.3	4.6	4.6	4.1	3.4	3.4					
1973	3.1	3.1	3.1	3.2	3.3	3.4	3.7	3.9	4.1	4.4	4.8	5.1	5.3	5.4	5.3	5.2	6.1	8.8				
1974	3.5	3.6	3.6	3.7	3.9	4.1	4.3	4.6	4.8	5.2	5.6	5.9	6.3	6.5	6.6	6.9	8.1	10.5	12.3			
1975	4.7	3.7	3.8	3.9	4.1	4.2	4.5	4.8	5.1	5.4	5.7	6.1	6.4	6.6	6.7	6.9	7.9	9.4	9.7	7.1		
1976	3.8	3.8	3.8	4.1	4.1	4.3	4.5	4.8	5.1	5.3	5.7	5.9	6.2	6.4	6.4	6.6	7.3	8.2	8.1	6.1	4.9	
1977	3.9	3.9	4.1	4.1	4.3	4.4	4.7	4.9	5.1	5.5	5.8	6.1	6.3	6.4	6.5	6.6	7.2	8.1	7.7	6.3	5.8	6.8
1978	4.1	4.2	4.2	4.4	4.5	4.7	4.9	5.2	5.4	5.7	6.1	6.2	6.5	6.7	6.8	6.9	7.4	8.1	8.1	6.9	6.9	7.9
1979	4.5	4.5	4.6	4.8	3.9	5.1	5.4	5.6	5.9	6.2	6.5	6.7	7.1	7.3	7.4	7.6	8.1	8.8	8.8	8.2	8.4	9.6
1980	4.8	4.9	4.9	5.1	5.3	5.5	5.7	6.1	6.2	6.6	6.9	7.1	7.5	7.7	7.8	8.1	8.6	9.3	9.3	8.9	9.2	10.3
1981	4.9	5.1	5.1	5.3	5.4	5.6	5.9	6.1	6.4	6.7	7.1	7.3	7.6	7.8	7.9	8.1	8.6	9.2	9.3	8.9	9.2	10.1
1982	4.9	5.1	5.1	5.2	5.4	5.5	5.8	6.1	6.3	6.5	6.8	7.1	7.3	7.5	7.6	7.8	8.2	8.7	8.7	8.2	8.4	9.1
1983	4.9	4.9	5.1	5.1	5.3	5.5	5.7	5.9	6.1	6.4	6.7	6.8	7.1	7.2	7.3	7.5	7.8	8.2	8.2	7.7	7.8	8.2
1984	4.8	4.9	5.1	5.1	5.2	5.4	5.6	5.8	6.1	6.3	6.5	6.7	6.9	7.1	7.1	7.2	7.5	7.9	7.8	7.4	7.4	7.7
1985	4.8	4.9	4.9	5.1	5.2	5.3	5.5	5.7	5.9	6.2	6.4	6.5	6.7	68	6.9	7.1	7.2	7.5	7.4	7.1	7.1	7.2
1986	4.7	4.7	4.8	4.9	5.1	5.3	5.4	5.5	5.7	5.9	6.1	6.2	6.4	6.5	6.5	6.6	6.8	7.1	6.9	6.5	6.5	6.6
1987	4.7	4.7	4.8	4.9	5.1	5.1	5.3	5.5	5.7	5.8	6.1	6.2	6.3	6.4	6.4	6.5	6.7	6.9	6.8	6.3	6.3	6.4
1988	4.7	4.7	4.8	4.9	5.1	5.1	5.3	5.4	5.6	5.8	6.1	6.1	6.2	6.3	6.3	6.4	6.5	6.7	6.6	6.2	6.1	6.2
1989	4.7	4.7	4.8	4.9	5.1	5.1	5.3	5.4	5.6	5.7	5.9	6.1	6.1	6.2	6.2	6.3	6.4	6.6	6.5	6.1	6.1	6.1
1990	4.7	4.7	4.8	4.9	5.1	5.1	5.3	5.4	5.6	5.8	5.9	6.1	6.1	6.2	6.2	6.3	6.4	6.6	6.5	6.1	6.1	6.1
1991	4.7	4.7	4.8	4.8	4.9	5.1	5.2	5.4	5.5	5.7	5.8	5.9	6.1	6.1	6.1	6.1	6.2	6.4	6.3	5.9	5.8	5.9
1992	4.6	4.7	4.7	4.8	4.9	5.1	5.1	5.3	5.4	5.6	5.7	5.8	5.9	5.9	5.9	6.1	6.1	6.2	6.1	5.7	5.7	5.7
1993	4.6	4.6	4.6	4.7	4.8	4.9	5.1	5.2	5.3	5.5	5.6	5.7	5.8	5.8	5.8	5.8	5.9	6.1	5.9	5.6	5.5	5.5
1994	4.5	4.6	4.6	4.7	4.8	4.9	5.1	5.1	5.2	5.4	5.5	5.6	5.7	5.7	5.7	5.7	5.8	5.9	5.8	5.4	5.4	5.4
1995	4.5	4.5	4.5	4.6	4.7	4.8	4.9	5.1	5.1	5.3	5.4	5.4	5.5	5.6	5.5	5.5	5.6	5.7	5.6	5.3	5.2	5.2
1996	4.4	4.5	4.5	4.6	4.7	4.7	4.9	5.1	5.1	4.2	5.3	5.4	5.5	5.5	5.5	5.5	5.6	5.5	5.2	5.1	5.1	
1997	4.4	4.4	4.4	4.5	4.6	4.7	4.8	4.9	5.1	5.1	5.2	5.3	5.3	5.4	5.3	5.3	5.4	5.5	5.3	5.1	5.1	5.1

1978	1979	1980	1981	1982	1983	1984	1985	1986	1987	1988	1989	1990	1991	1992	1993	1994	1995	1996	1997
9.1																			
11.1	13.2																		
11.5	12.8	12.4																	
10.9	11.5	10.6	8.9																
9.4	9.5	8.3	6.4	3.9															
8.5	8.4	7.2	5.5	3.8	3.8														
7.8	7.6	6.5	5.1	3.9	3.9	4.1													
7.3	7.1	6.1	4.8	3.8	3.8	3.8	3.7												
6.6	6.3	5.3	4.2	3.3	3.1	2.9	2.4	1.1											
6.4	6.1	5.2	4.2	3.5	3.4	3.3	3.1	2.7	4.4										
6.2	5.9	5.1	4.3	3.6	3.6	3.5	3.4	3.3	4.4	4.4									
6.1	5.8	5.1	4.3	3.7	3.7	3.7	3.6	3.6	4.5	4.5	4.6								
6.1	5.8	5.2	4.5	4.1	4.1	4.1	4.1	4.1	4.9	5.1	5.3	6.1							
5.8	5.6	5.1	4.3	3.9	3.9	3.9	3.9	3.9	4.5	4.5	4.6	4.6	3.1						
5.6	5.4	4.8	4.2	3.8	3.8	3.8	3.8	3.8	4.2	4.2	4.2	4.1	3.1	2.9					
5.5	5.2	4.7	4.1	3.7	3.7	3.7	3.7	3.7	4.1	4.1	3.9	3.7	2.9	2.8	2.7				
5.3	5.1	4.5	4.1	3.6	3.6	3.6	3.6	3.5	3.9	3.8	3.7	3.5	2.8	2.8	2.7	2.7			
5.1	4.9	4.4	3.9	3.6	35	3.5	3.5	3.4	3.7	3.6	3.5	3.3	2.8	2.7	2.6	2.6	2.4		
5.1	4.8	4.3	3.9	3.5	3.5	3.5	3.4	3.4	3.7	3.6	3.5	3.3	2.8	2.8	2.8	2.8	2.9	3.3	
4.9	4.7	4.2	3.7	3.4	3.4	3.4	3.3	3.3	3.5	3.4	3.3	3.1	2.7	2.6	2.6	2.5	2.5	2.5	1.7